D0039073

Pocket
DUBAI

TOP SIGHTS • LOCAL LIFE • MADE EASY

Josephine Quintero

In This Book

QuickStart Guide

Your keys to understanding the city – we help you decide what to do and how to do it

Need to Know
Tips for a smooth trip

Neighbourhoods
What's where

Explore Dubai

The best things to see and do, neighbourhood by neighbourhood

Top Sights
Make the most of your visit

Local Life
The insider's city

The Best of Dubai

The city's highlights in handy lists to help you plan

Best Walks
See the city on foot

Dubai's Best...
The best experiences

Survival Guide

Tips and tricks for a seamless, hassle-free city experience

Getting Around
Travel like a local

Essential Information
Including where to stay

Our selection of the city's best places to eat, drink and experience:

◉ **Sights**

✖ **Eating**

🍺 **Drinking**

✪ **Entertainment**

🔒 **Shopping**

These symbols give you the vital information for each listing:

☎ Telephone Numbers	✿ Family-Friendly
⊙ Opening Hours	🐾 Pet-Friendly
P Parking	🚌 Bus
⊗ Nonsmoking	🚢 Ferry
@ Internet Access	Ⓜ Metro
📶 Wi-Fi Access	Ⓢ Subway
🥗 Vegetarian Selection	🚋 Tram
📖 English-Language Menu	🚆 Train

Find each listing quickly on maps for each neighbourhood:

Bar Hemingway

16 🍺 Map p233, B2

Legend has it that Hemi self, wielding a machine rate this timber-pan ered bar during showpiece is a en by Papa ar town. Dress s.com; Hôtel Rit ⊙6.30pm-2a

---

Lonely Planet's Dubai

Lonely Planet Pocket Guides are designed to get you straight to the heart of the city.

Inside you'll find all the must-see sights, plus tips to make your visit to each one really memorable. We've split the city into easy-to-navigate neighbourhoods and provided clear maps so you'll find your way around with ease. Our expert authors have searched out the best of the city: walks, food, nightlife and shopping, to name a few. Because you want to explore, our 'Local Life' pages will take you to some of the most exciting areas to experience the real Dubai.

And of course you'll find all the practical tips you need for a smooth trip: itineraries for short visits, how to get around, and how much to tip the guy who serves you a drink at the end of a long day's exploration. It's your guarantee of a really great experience.

Our Promise

You can trust our travel information because Lonely Planet authors visit the places we write about, each and every edition. We never accept freebies for positive coverage, so you can rely on us to tell it like it is.

QuickStart Guide 7

Explore Dubai 21

Worth a Trip:

The Best of Dubai 125

Dubai's Best Walks

Dubai's Best...

Survival Guide 145

QuickStart Guide

Welcome to Dubai

This is a destination that is original, extreme and full of scope and surprises. Be prepared to be spoiled rotten by excellent restaurants, pampering spas, New York–style shopping, luxurious hotels and a legendary nightlife. Or opt for a more locally flavoured trip, with atmospheric souqs, *abra* (water taxi) rides, edgy art galleries and a corner-kiosk kebab. The choice is wonderfully and conveniently yours.

The coastline of Jumeirah (p58) and the Dubai skyline
JEAN-PIERRE LESCOURRET/LONELY PLANET IMAGES ©

Dubai
Top Sights

Dubai Museum (p40)

This remarkable museum is a must-see attraction in Dubai, not only for the evocative historic building in which it is housed, but also for the fascinating exhibits.

Gold Souq (p24)

Head to Deira's Gold Souq, with its dazzling jewellery and shimmering gems displayed in rows of shops set among wooden-latticed lanes. It positively bustles with shoppers.

Madinat Jumeirah (p68)

Marvel at the mythical old Arabian architecture at Madinat Jumeirah, with its mesmerising shopping, entertainment and restaurants set around picture-postcard Venetian-style canals.

Dubai Mall (p82)

Hang on to those purse strings or give in to temptation at Dubai Mall, an extraordinary place with more shops than any other mall in the world, and a whole lot more besides. It's also home to a three-storey aquarium.

Abu Dhabi (p118)

Dubai's neighbouring emirate is well worth visiting for its wonderful beach, impressive museums and fabulous Taj Mahal–style Grand Mosque, one of the most magnificent in the entire Arabian world. There's great dining and shopping, too.

Dubai
Local Life

Insider tips to help you find the real city

It is all too easy to luxuriate in the faultless opulence and luxury here, but if you delve beyond the anonymous gloss, you'll discover that there really is an intrinsic feel to the place that is uniquely, and memorably, Dubai.

Let's Do Brunch... (p102)

▶ Good value
▶ Diverse cuisine

It's one of the most agreeable traditions here: weekly brunch at any one of a growing number of superb restaurants that lay on a palate-pleasing buffet (with or without alcohol) at an all-inclusive price. Many are great for hard-to-please families and friends, with extras like children's entertainment and stellar views.

Al-Quoz: An Edgy Urban Art District (p84)

▶ Inspiring
▶ Something different

Discover some of the United Arab Emirate's most cutting-edge galleries hidden away from the main tourist sights in an industrial area south of Sheikh Zayed Road. Exploring in among the nondescript buildings and anonymous warehouses here can unearth some very exciting contemporary art spaces, featuring work primarily by local and Middle Eastern artists.

Desert Safaris (p46)

▶ Adventure
▶ Breathtaking scenery

Dubai's Bedouin heritage is extremely strong, and its people retain a powerful affinity for the desert. You can get a taste of a traditional desert-dweller's lifestyle by joining a desert safari. Although the safaris are obviously geared towards tourists, the experience of enjoying traditional cuisine and entertainment in the middle of the moonlit desert will doubtless be memorable.

Sharjah's Charms & Culture (p122)

▶ Tradition
▶ Culture

Neighbouring emirate Sharjah may not dazzle with the modernity of Dubai, but its cultural sights are varied and fascinating, with quality museums, galleries, festivals and theatres. Add to this some lively souqs, where you can indulge your souvenir cravings, and you've got a fascinating destination that's well worth a visit.

Visitors on a desert safari (p46)

Minaret and wind towers, Bur Dubai

Other great experiences and insights to help you enjoy Dubai like a local:

Bastakia Tours (p44)

Bargaining at the Souq (p48)

Vegetarian Restaurants (p74)

The Friday Mall Experience (p98)

Multi-Ethnic Eats (p32)

The Pashmina (p35)

Celebrity Chefs Come (and Go) (p111)

Red Carpet Viewing (p116)

Dubai
Day Planner

Day One

Head for Bur Dubai's historic Bastakia Quarter and a leisurely breakfast in the tranquil walled garden of the **Basta Art Cafe** (p48). Pop next door to check out the exhibitions at the inviting **Majlis Gallery** (p46) before making your way to the Creek via the colourful hurly-burly of **Hindi Lane** (p44). Explore the surrounding souq stalls indulging in some healthy banter and barter, taking time off for freshly squeezed mango juice at one of the hole-in-the-wall cafes.

Enjoy tasty Middle Eastern dishes during a late lunch overlooking the water at **Bait Al Wakeel** (p48), before doubling back to the air-conditioned **Dubai Museum** (p40) during the hottest part of the day. Then, in the late afternoon, hire an *abra* (water taxi) for a picturesque **creek cruise** (p30).

Hop off your boat in Deira and explore the glittery **Gold Souq** (p24) and the aromatic **Spice Souq** (p29), before enjoying an amble through the Shindagha area and the **Heritage & Diving Villages** (p44). Follow this up with a creekside candlelit dinner at **Kan Zaman** (p49).

Day Two

It's time to head for the world's largest shopping centre: **Dubai Mall** (p82). Get here right at 10am when it opens and get into gold-credit-card mode by grabbing a pew at the swanky **Emporio Armani Caffé** (p90) for a coffee and croissant. Visit the superb **Dubai Aquarium** (p83) then indulge in a dose of retail therapy followed by a lunch of Middle Eastern delights at **Zaatar W Zeit** (p92).

It's time for a cultural fix, so head for the nearby Financial District and mosey around the superb galleries at **Gate Village** (p88). Double back to the Mall and cross the bridge to the flamboyant **Souq al-Bahar** (p88) to explore the souvenir shops in the shadow of the rocket-like **Burj Khalifa** (p88). Head to the latter late in the afternoon for a trip to the observation deck 'At the Top' and the best views in town.

Grab a seat on the terrace at **Baker & Spice** (p90) for a healthy, delicious dinner and front-row views of the **Dancing Fountains** (p83). Finish up your day by joining the cool cats for some of the finest blues and jazz in town at the **Blue Bar** (p96).

Short on time?
We've arranged Dubai's must-sees into these day-by-day itineraries to make sure you see the very best of the city in the time you have available.

Day Three

Start the day bright and early in bustling Deira, and take a trip back in time at the **Al-Ahmadiya School** (p28) and **Heritage House** (p28). Inhale those pungent *attar* aromas at the **Perfume Souq** (p28), before wandering along the colourful **dhow wharves** (p28) and enjoying a Mongolian hotpot lunch at the **Xiao Wei Yang** (p30).

If you can take the heat, taxi it to the **Jumeirah Beach Park** (p62) for a sunbed flop and a dip in the sea. Once you've brushed off the sand, continue along the coast to souq-styled **Madinat Jumeirah** (p68) for its excellent shopping and architecture.

When it's 'wine o'clock', head to **The Agency** (p74) for a glass of chilled chardonnay, and follow this up with an *abra* ride to **Pierchic** (p74) for a romantic dinner under the stars.

Day Four

Plan to turn up at 10am sharp for a tour of the **Jumeirah Mosque** (p62). Follow this with a coffee and slice of legendary carrot cake at the **Lime Tree Cafe** (p62). Drop by the Village Mall and the sassy boutique **S*uce** (p64) before hopping in a taxi to the **Mall of the Emirates** (p116).

Have lunch at **Sezzam** (p103); its global choices will suit the fussiest of families. It's the hottest time of the day, so hit the snow at **Ski Dubai** (p107), then cruise the shops, being sure not to miss one-stop fashion shop **Aizone** (p117). Hop on the metro or taxi it to Dubai Marina.

Enjoy an amble along the **Walk at JBR** (p106), plus a coffee or ice-cream break. Spend an hour or two kicking back on the beach here, before hopping on the monorail to Palm Jumeirah and dipping into the stunning underwater labyrinth of the **Lost Chambers** (p106). Zip back to the mainland and the exotic surroundings of the **Buddha Bar** (p113), before enjoying a spicy Mexican meal (and margarita or two) at celebrity chef–driven **Maya** (p111). Head up to the rooftop bar here for a late-night cocktail in sumptuous, romantic surrounds.

Need to Know

For more information, see Survival Guide (p145).

Currency
United Arab Emirates (UAE) dirhams (Dh)

Language
Arabic and English

Visas
Citizens of 34 countries, including nearly all of western Europe, get free 30-day visas on arrival in the UAE. Visas are nonrenewable.

Money
ATMs widely available. Credit cards accepted in most hotels, restaurants and shops.

Mobile Phones
You can buy a pay-as-you-go mobile with credit for as little as Dh125. Alternatively, local SIM cards are widely available.

Time
Dubai is four hours ahead of GMT. The time does not change during the summer.

Plugs & Adaptors
Electrical current is 220V. British-style three-pin wall sockets are standard. North American visitors will require an adaptor and a transformer.

Tipping
Not generally expected in taxis or restaurants. Service charges are added to restaurant bills. Tip porters around Dh2.

① Before You Go

Your Daily Budget

Budget less than Dh600
► Budget hotel room Dh300-Dh400
► Excellent supermarkets for self-caterers
► Cheap museum entrance fees, free public beaches

Midrange Dh600-Dh1200
► Double room Dh500
► Two-course meal in good midrange restaurant Dh125-Dh200, plus wine
► Top attractions and sights average Dh100

Top end over Dh1200
► Four-star hotel room from Dh1000
► Fine dining for dinner from Dh800
► Bar tab for wine and beer from Dh300

Useful Websites

Lonely Planet (www.lonelyplanet.com /dubai) Destination information, hotel bookings, traveller forum and more.

Dubai Tourism (www.dubaitourism.ae) Official tourism site of the Dubai government.

Dubai Lime (www.dubailime.com) Classifieds, culture, events and features.

Advance Planning

Three months before Double check visa regulations as these can alter without prior warning. Check date of Ramadan, which changes annually.

One month before Reserve a table at a top restaurant. Check concert-venue websites for what's on during your stay.

One week before Check average daytime temperature.

2 Arriving in Dubai

The metro, buses and taxis to central Dubai are all convenient modes of transport to/ from the airport. If you are staying at a four- or five-star hotel, check with your hotel whether an airport transfer is available.

✈ From Dubai International Airport

Destination	Best Transport
Metro stops throughout the city	Metro Red Line from Terminals 1 & 3
Al Sabkha Bus Station, Deira	RTA Bus 401
Al-Ghubaiba Bus Station, Bur Dubai	RTA Bus 402

At the Airport

Dubai International Airport The arrivals hall has several ATMs and a couple of currency-exchange outlets, plus car hire and a tourist information desk. The airport has several restaurants in the departure lounge as well as a large duty-free store and shops. There is also an on-site hotel, Dubai International Hotel, with two locations: one on the arrivals level in Terminal 1, and the other in Terminal 3, on levels five and six. Rooms are available at hourly rates, upon request.

3 Getting Around

Most visitors here use taxis to get around as they are relatively inexpensive. It is important to realise that the drivers navigate not via addresses but via landmarks, so make sure you know exactly where you are going. The metro is an inexpensive, speedy and comfortable mode of transport and, at the major sights, like Dubai Mall, metro stops will coordinate with feeder buses to connect with the final destination. Before you hop aboard the metro or a bus, you must purchase a rechargeable Nol card available from ticket offices at any metro station and some bus stations, plus ticket-vending machines. Check www.nol.ae for more details.

Ⓜ Metro

There are two metro lines. The Red Line runs from near Dubai International Airport to Jebel Ali. The Green Line links the Dubai Airport Free Zone with Dubai Healthcare City.

🚕 Taxi

There are several taxi companies operating throughout the city and, aside from around key sights and the shopping malls, they are generally easy to flag down. There are taxi ranks outside shopping malls and hotels.

🚌 Bus

There is a network of 79 bus routes. Buses can be overcrowded and slow, although long-distance buses generally have direct routes and are adequately comfortable.

Dubai's Neighbourhoods

Madinat Jumeirah

New Dubai (p100)
A sumptuous marina, that famous 'Palm', ski slopes in a mall and some of the finest UAE hotels, restaurants and night spots.

Madinat Jumeirah & Around (p66)
Great for families, this area has superb beaches, restaurants, water parks and shopping for souvenirs, plus that iconic Burj.

◉ Top Sights
Madinat Jumeirah

Worth a Trip
◉ Top Sights
Abu Dhabi

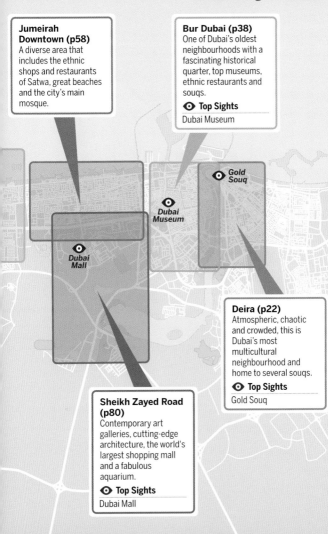

Jumeirah Downtown (p58)
A diverse area that includes the ethnic shops and restaurants of Satwa, great beaches and the city's main mosque.

Bur Dubai (p38)
One of Dubai's oldest neighbourhoods with a fascinating historical quarter, top museums, ethnic restaurants and souqs.

⊙ **Top Sights**
Dubai Museum

Gold Souq

Dubai Museum

Dubai Mall

Deira (p22)
Atmospheric, chaotic and crowded, this is Dubai's most multicultural neighbourhood and home to several souqs.

⊙ **Top Sights**
Gold Souq

Sheikh Zayed Road (p80)
Contemporary art galleries, cutting-edge architecture, the world's largest shopping mall and a fabulous aquarium.

⊙ **Top Sights**
Dubai Mall

Explore
Dubai

Worth a Trip

An *abra* (water taxi) on the Creek (p30)
GIOVANNI SIMEONE/4CORNERS ©

Explore

Deira

Deira is an earthy, atmospheric neighbourhood and the historic heart of the city. The most fascinating area is creekside Al-Ras, where colourful wooden boats unload their boxes of wares to be sold at the nearby souqs. The surrounding streets are lined with small shops and ethnic restaurants. It's a world away from the sophisticated new city piercing the clouds at the other end of town.

The Sights in a Day

First, visit Deira's seductive **Spice Souq** (p29), enjoying tantalising aromas and some good-humoured banter. Stop for a fresh fruit juice and watch the *abras* (water taxis) crossing the Creek before escaping the escalating heat at the **Heritage House** (p28) museum and adjacent **Al-Ahmadiya School** (p28) historic schoolhouse.

It's time for some sustenance, so depending on your energy levels, either grab a kebab on the go or take a taxi to the **Glasshouse Mediterranean Brasserie** (p31) for a leisurely lunch overlooking the Creek. Stroll off that calorific dessert at the Dhow Wharfage across the way before going for gold and getting glittered up at the **Gold Souq** (p24) – another taxi ride away. Spend any time left getting happily lost in the surrounding shop-lined streets, stopping for a cup of punchy Arabic coffee when you start to flag.

The best place to flash those new baubles is at **The Terrace** (p33) waterside bar. Drink in the view, sip the champagne and sample the caviar before enjoying Asian delights at the **Thai Kitchen** (p32), a few steps away. If you have any energy left, head for **QDs** (p33), overlooking the romantic moonlit Creek, for some sultry dancing under the stars.

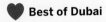

Top Sights
Gold Souq (p24)

Best of Dubai

Eating
Traiteur (p30)

Xiao Wei Yang (p31)

Shabestan (p31)

Drinking
The Terrace (p33)

QDs (p33)

Non-Souq Shopping
Deira City Centre (p35)

Getting There

Ⓜ **Metro** The most convenient option is the metro. The main central stops are Al Rigga, Union and Deira City Centre (Red Line).

Ⓜ **Metro** Other useful metro stops are Al Ras, Palm Deira and Baniyas square (Green Line).

⚓ **Ferry** The area is also served by *abra* and water bus from Bur Dubai's Abra and Water Bus Station; this is the most scenic option.

Top Sights
Gold Souq

All that glitters is gold (and occasionally silver) at this colourful market. At any given time over 25 tonnes of gold is for sale in Dubai, much of it at the Gold Souq, one of the world's largest gold markets. Literally hundreds of stores overflow with every kind of jewellery imaginable, ranging from modest diamond earrings to over-the-top golden Indian wedding necklaces. Even if you're not in the market for bling, a stroll through the covered arcades here is a must.

◉ Map p26, B1

www.dubaitourism.ae

Sikkat al-Khail St

🕘10am-1pm & 3-10pm

Ⓜ Palm Deira (Green Line)

Don't Miss

Going Fake

Not at the Gold Souq, we hasten to add. The gold sold here is strictly regulated and genuine, but the streets surrounding the souq are one of Dubai's busiest and most vibrant areas for selling counterfeit goods, such as watches, DVDs, bags, sunglasses and other similar must-have (or not) designer accessories. The quality varies, so check carefully before you dish out the dirhams – and bargain hard.

The Art of Bartering

Even if you are kind of uncomfortable with the idea, this is the place where you really need to indulge in a little good-humoured bargaining. Remember, it's expected and always reflected in that initial price. However, don't expect the dramatic variance that you find in other souqs; there is not so much leeway here. Start by knocking off 30% and work up from there.

The Extraordinary Golden Spectacle

You simply cannot prepare yourself for the overwhelming sight of this much gold. For most folk (unless they are gold traders or zillionaires), the most gold ever seen in one place is probably the local jeweller's shop back home. But here, the amount of glitter is truly mesmerising. It is a real one off. Feast your eyes (if you can take all that sparkle). Otherwise keep your shades firmly in place...

☑ Top Tips

▶ Get here early, or at least in the morning, to avoid the crowds.

▶ Credit cards are virtually always accepted, but you'll get a better price with cash.

▶ If you don't see anything you like, don't panic. Most shops will custom-make something to your own design.

▶ Don't rush! Remember, you don't have to make a decision on the spot. Consider carefully before you buy.

✕ Take a Break

For an earthy ethnic snack head to the **Ashwaq Cafeteria** (p32) for a juicy *shwarma* (meat sliced off a spit and stuffed in a pocket of pita-type bread with chopped tomatoes and garnish) and freshly squeezed mango juice.

If you fancy something a tad swisher, head for the sumptuous Hyatt Regency, home to several excellent restaurants: **Miyako** (p31) has tasty Japanese cuisine.

Dubai International Airport

44A

13A

19B

HOR AL-ANZ

Al-Ittihad Rd

22B

Airport Rd

35A
33B
33A
28C
30

28B

23A 1/A
2
12B
21A

31A

37
8B
4
39B

Abu Bakar al-Siddiq Rd

1A
9
6
10A
7A
5A
8
18
11A
9A
1A

12B
14
13B
8B
11B
16

22A

Al-Muraqqabat Rd

22B

26B
29
26C
45B
43

Al-Rigga Rd

1C

28A

Airport Rd

6B
25
27

47

AA

2

RIGGA

Al Rigga Ⓜ

23D
36A
34A
40C
34C

41C

42A

38

9
15
10

12B

14

17

Ⓜ16

Sheikh Rashid Rd

4B

40B

Al-Maktoum Rd

Clock Tower Roundabout

PORT SAEED

Deira City Centre Ⓜ

Dubai Creek Golf Course

Ⓧ13

Baniyas Rd

15 Ⓧ9

5 Ⓞ Dhow Wharves

Al-Maktoum Bridge

Floating Bridge

Creekside Park

Ⓜ Oud Metha

Al-Seef Rd

Riyadh St

OUD METHA

Dubai Healthcare City Ⓜ

E

D

C

B

A

5

6

7

8

Sights

Deira Covered Souq
MARKET

1 Map p26, B2

Don't be surprised if, just as you think you have a handle on where you are here, you get lost all over again. Deceptively large and disorienting, this warren of narrow lanes is lined with small shops selling everything from lurid textiles to plastic coffee pots. If you get worn out by the shopping, just take in the captivating surroundings. (btwn Al-Sabkha Rd, 67 St & Naif Rd)

Perfume Souq
MARKET

2 Map p26, B2

Several blocks of perfume shops stretching south of the Gold Souq hardly warrants the title 'souq', yet these bustling stores sell a staggering range of Arabic *attars* (perfumes), *oud* (fragrant wood) and incense burners. More fascinating than the perfumes is the perfume-buying ritual – just watch the burka-covered ladies waft the smoke from burning *oud* under their *abeyyas* (full-length black robes worn by women) as they sample the pungent aromas. (Sikkat al-Khail St)

Heritage House
MUSEUM

3 Map p26, B1

Get a glimpse inside a wealthy pearl merchant's former residence. Built in 1890, the home, near the Gold Souq, belonged to Sheikh Ahmed bin Dalmouk, whose son established Al-Ahmadiya School next door. Sit back on cushions under the central Bedouin-style tent and enjoy coffee and traditional snacks, like *loqmat* (fried flour balls with rose water and honey) for just Dh3. (Al-Ahmadiya St; admission free; ⊘8am-7.30pm Sat-Thu, 2.30-7.30pm Fri)

Al-Ahmadiya School
MUSEUM

4 Map p26, B1

An exquisite courtyard house with gorgeous decorative gypsum panels, Dubai's oldest school was built in 1912 by Sheikh Mohammed bin Ahmed bin Dalmouk. Students paid a few rupees to attend, with the sheikh sponsoring poorer students, a practice that continues today. (Al-Ahmadiya St; admission free; ⊘8am-7.30pm Sat-Thu, 2.30-7.30pm Fri)

Dhow Wharves
HARBOUR

5 Map p26, B5

Dhows have docked at the Creek since the 1830s, when the Maktoums established a free-trade port, luring merchants away from Persia. Today's dhows head to Iran, Iraq, Pakistan, Oman, India, Yemen, Somalia and

---

☑ Top Tip

Cash Talks

If you are making a purchase at one of the Deira souqs (aside from the Gold Souq), you will probably have to pay in cash as credit cards are not widely accepted, so make sure you have plenty of small denomination notes and coins handy.

JOHN ELK III/LONELY PLANET IMAGES ©

Exhibit at Al-Ahmadiya School

Sudan, and you'll see them precariously loaded with everything from air conditioners to chewing gum to car tyres. An evening stroll here is highly recommended. (Baniyas Rd)

Naif Souq
MARKET

 6 Map p26, C2

More like a typical Middle Eastern bazaar than the Deira Covered Souq, Naif Souq is where Emiratis and African expats like to shop for everything from fake Chanel *shaylas* (black veils or headscarves) to cheap children's clothes and toys. Sometimes more interesting than the shopping is the amazing insight this souq gives into the lives of the locals. (btwn Naif South St, 9a St & Deira St)

Fish Market
MARKET

7 Map p26, C1

Shrimp the size of bananas, metre-long kingfish and mountains of blue crabs are among the treasures of the sea hawked at Dubai's largest fish market. (Beware: the smell can be overpowering.) Come early in the morning if you can. After you've had your fish full, pop next door to the fruit and vegetable market: the small green mangos and bananas are grown locally. (Al-Khaleej Rd; ⊙7am-1.30pm & 4-10pm)

Spice Souq
MARKET

8 Map p26, B2

The Spice Souq is possibly Dubai's most atmospheric and certainly its

Understand
Creek Crossing

Dubai Creek meanders for some 15km, dividing Deira from Bur Dubai. There are four ways across the Creek: the 13-lane Business Bay Bridge near Dubai Festival City; a six-lane Floating Bridge (open 6am to 10pm) near Creekside Park; the 13-lane Al-Garhoud Bridge, south of Dubai Creek Golf Course; and Al-Shindagha Tunnel, near the mouth of the Creek (open to both vehicles and pedestrians).

Using public transport, you now have three options for crossing the Creek. The fastest and easiest is Dubai Metro's Red Line, which runs below the Creek between Union and Khalid bin al-Waleed stations. The most atmospheric way to get across, though, is a Dh1 ride aboard a traditional *abra* that links the Bur Dubai and Deira souqs in a quick five minutes. In summer, you might prefer the air-conditioned comfort of the water buses, which cost just a few dirhams more.

Also consider hiring an *abra* for your own personal cruising along (and across) the creek (Dh100 for one hour), which is great for sightseeing at your own pace.

most fragrant souq. Be transported to the heart of Arabia among the stalls piled high with spices: cloves, cardamom, cinnamon, Iranian saffron, huge vanilla pods and rocks of salt, together with the more unusual frankincense, baskets full of dried rose heads, preserved lemons, hibiscus and dried herbs used in natural remedies. (btwn Baniyas Rd, Al-Sabkha Rd & Al-Abra St)

Eating

Traiteur   FRENCH $$$
9 🍽 Map p26, B8

A meal at Traiteur is pure drama, both on the plate and in the striking 14m-high dining room with origami wall features and theatrical lighting. Watch a small army of cooks in toques in the show kitchen toil over classic French brasserie fare. Ask the sommelier to help you choose from the 4200-bottle wine cellar, one of Dubai's largest. (☎04-317 2222; www.dubai.park.hyatt.com; Park Hyatt Dubai; mains Dh130-190; 🕖7pm-midnight)

Xiao Wei Yang   CHINESE $
10 🍽 Map p26, B3

For hotpot novices, this is how it works: choose a base, which bubbles happily on a hotplate on the table. Create a combination of satay, garlic, coriander, chilli and/or other spices. Select around three ingredients – like crab, tofu, shitake mushrooms or spicy lamb – to cook in the cauldron before dipping into your spicy concoction. Little atmosphere; you're here for the food. (Baniyas Rd; hotpots from Dh35; ☺noon-2am)

Shabestan
PERSIAN $$$

11 ✕ Map p26, C3

Shabestan is a top Persian restaurant. At dinner time, the window-lined dining room reveals a panorama of glittering lights over the Creek. Start with a smoky *mizra ghasemi* (aubergine dip with tomatoes and egg), move on to *fesenjan-ba morgh* (roast chicken in a pomegranate sauce) and save room for the vermicelli ice cream with saffron and rose water. (✆04-205 7333; www.radissonblue.com; Radisson Blu Hotel, Baniyas Rd, mains Dh90-135)

Miyako
JAPANESE $$$

12 ✕ Map p26, D1

Revamped with the old Hyatt's makeover, this consistently outstanding Japanese restaurant has style to match the flavours on offer. Tuna and salmon are reliable options for the sushi and sashimi, but there are far more tempting choices on offer – try the seafood hotpot *kaminabe* and *kakuni* (braised pork belly). (✆04-209 1222; Hyatt Regency, off Al-Khaleej Rd; mains from Dh90)

Glasshouse Mediterranean Brasserie
MEDITERRANEAN $$$

13 ✕ Map p26, C5

Glasshouse is one of Dubai's most accomplished brasserie-style restaurants, with, as the name suggests, vast picture windows overlooking the Creek. The comfort-food menu offers fresh takes on classics, like pea and

---

Understand
Wining & Dining

If you enjoy a glass with dinner, then you will catch on fast that this is not standard practice in Dubai. The bottom line is that there are essentially two types of restaurants here: the hotel restaurant and the independent. Only hotels are licensed to serve alcohol, which is why they house the city's most popular dining rooms, particularly for Westerners. Alas, because they fall under the umbrellas of giant corporate hotel chains, many of these top-end spots lack the uniqueness and eccentricity you would find in a first-class Western restaurant.

Head to the independent restaurant when you want local atmosphere and traditional cuisine; head to the hotels when you want splash and panache – and a big glass of vino to wash it down. Unsurprisingly, the top bars and clubs are, overall, also found in the city's hotels.

✓ Top Tip
Get Lost

Some of the most fascinating parts of Deira aren't home to a single tourist attraction worth recommending, but are brimming with the soul the city is so frequently accused of lacking. Dubai is a safe city; there aren't any no-go areas, and even the scariest-looking alleyways will be quite harmless. Be spontaneous. Put away the maps for a couple of hours and follow your instincts and sense of adventure: the area between Naif Rd and Al-Khaleej Rd is a good place to start...

broad-bean risotto and a tiger prawns bruschetta with red chilli, garlic and lemon. Come on Monday and Wednesday and get drinks for just Dh1 with two courses. (☎04-227 1111; Hilton Dubai Creek, Baniyas Rd; mains Dh95-110)

The Thai Kitchen   THAI $$$

You'll find this stylish restaurant near Traiteur (see 9 ⊗ Map p26, B8). It's a worthwhile trip to northeastern Thailand, former home of chef Khun Supathra (one of Dubai's few female chefs). Try the tangy, refreshing grapefruit or green papaya salads as well as the beef with hot basil, then down one of the fabulous spicy cocktail creations. (☎04-602 1234; Park Hyatt Dubai; mains Dh100; ⊙7pm-midnight daily plus 12.30-4pm Fri)

Ashwaq Cafeteria   IRANIAN $

14 ⊗ Map p26, B2

Located in a prime people-watching spot at the junction of Al-Soor and Sikka Al-Khail, this is not much more than a kiosk with a few outside tables serving up excellent *shwarma*, best washed down with a fresh fruit juice. Try the mango or avocado juice for a real tastebud treat. (Sikka Al-Khail Rd; shwarma Dh5)

YUM!   ASIAN $$

You will find this restaurant near Shabestan (see 11 ⊗ Map p26, C3) at the Radisson Blu Hotel. Yum! serves up tasty Far Eastern fare fresh from its open kitchen. The *tom kha gai* (chicken and coconut soup) and wok specials such as *char kway teow* (stir-fried noodles) are excellent. The location is convenient if you're

◎ Local Life
Multi-Ethnic Eats

To sample some of Dubai's best ethnic cooking, hit the backstreets of Deira and eat beside the expat workers who've imported their culinary traditions to Dubai. A good place to start is the **Afghan Kebab House** (Map p26, C2; off Deira St; mains Dh15-35; ⊙11am-1am), which serves big hunks of meat – lamb, beef, chicken – charred on foot-long skewers and served with rice and bread. Eat with your hands. Delicious!

wandering along the Creek – or in a hurry: you can be in and out in half an hour. (Radisson Blu Hotel, Baniyas Rd; mains Dh45-65, ⊘noon-1am)

Drinking

The Terrace   LOUNGE

After your meal at nearby Traiteur (see 9  Map p26, B3), head here for the view of the boats and the DJ spinning chill-out grooves. This waterside lounge bar specialises in vodka, champagne, caviar and oysters and is a wonderful place to while away a few indulgent hours on that last night in Dubai. Head here earlier in the trip and you'll be making plans to stay. (Park Hyatt Dubai; ⊘noon-late)

QDs   LOUNGE

15 🎵 Map p26, B8

Sit and watch the lighted dhows floating by while sipping cosmos at this always-fun Creekside lounge shaped like a giant circle. The main action is on the raised centre ring with oriental carpets and cushions. It's a sublime spot for *sheesha* (water pipe used to smoke tobacco) and beers during the cooler winter months, particularly on a moonlit night, when the Creek looks especially magical. (Dubai Creek Golf & Yacht Club; ⊘6pm-3am)

Traditional Arabic coffee

Ku Bu   COCKTAIL BAR

Kick back with a few cocktails while tapping your toes to some funky tunes provided by the house DJ. This intimate bar has an Afro-cool interior and secluded seating areas concealed by plush drapes. A good choice for drinks before or after dinner at one of the Radisson Blu's terrific restaurants, like Shabestan (see 11  Map p26, C3). (Radisson Blu Hotel, Baniyas Rd; ⊘7pm-3am)

Café Havana   CAFE

The city centre's most popular cafe, this sprawling, stylish place in the Deira City Centre (see 16 🔒 Map p26, C8) provides a rare chance for visitors to hang out with local Emirati guys who

☑ Top Tip

Juice Time

Deira is a great place to find freshly made juices. Try a creamy avocado juice if you can. Laced with honey and sprinkled with pistachios, it is a delicious (and nutritious) treat.

kick back here for hours chatting and cutting business deals. (Level II, Deira City Centre, Al-Garhoud Rd; ⊘8am-midnight)

Issimo

SPORTS BAR

Illuminated blue flooring, black-leather sofas and sleek chrome finishing lend a James Bond look to this sports-and-martini bar. If you're not into sports – or TV – you may find the giant screens distracting. Good for drinks before dining at the nearby Glasshouse Mediterranean Brasserie (see 13 ✕ Map p26, C5). (Hilton Dubai Creek, Baniyas Rd; ⊘ 11am-2am)

Entertainment

Vox

CINEMA

Catch the latest Hollywood block-busters, American indie flicks and the occasional European film at this popular state-of-the-art 11-screen complex at the Deira City Centre (see 16 🔒 Map p26, C8). (www.voxcinemas.com; Deira City Centre, Al-Garhoud Rd; tickets Dh45-50)

MIDDLE EAST/ALAMY ©

Pashminas in a Deira souq

Understand
The Pashmina

Women around the world adore pashminas – those feather-light cashmere shawls worn by the Middle East's best-dressed ladies. If you're shopping for a girlfriend or your mother, you can never go wrong with a pashmina. They come in hundreds of colours and styles – some beaded and embroidered, others with pompom edging – so you'll have no trouble finding one you like. But aside from setting it alight to make sure it doesn't melt (as polyester does), how can you be sure it's real? Here's the trick. Hold the fabric at its corner. Loop your index finger around it and squeeze hard. Now pull the fabric through. If it's polyester, it won't budge. If it's cashmere, it'll pull through – though the friction may give you a mild case of rope burn. Try it at home with a thin piece of polyester before you hit the shops; then try it with cashmere. You'll never be fooled again.

Amara   SPA

Dubai's top spa, at the Park Hyatt, has eight treatment suites, all with their own private walled garden complete with outdoor rain shower. Nonguests can enjoy a day pass or choose one of the treatments, which entitles you daylong use of the steam bath, sauna and pool. Choose your own background music, then lean back for a luxurious foot bath followed by your selected treatment. Consider combining your spa visit with a meal at the hotel's superb Traiteur restaurant (see 9 ✖ Map p26, B3). (🕿 04-602 1234; www.dubai.park.hyatt.com; Park Hyatt Dubai; day pass Mon-Fri Dh300, Sat & Sun Dh350)

Shopping
Deira City Centre   SHOPPING MALL
16 🔒 Map p26, C8

This is still one of Dubai's most popular malls, despite openings of glitzy megamalls such as the Dubai Mall. City Centre has an excellent range of shops, from smaller, locally run stores to international chains, plus food courts, cinemas and an amusement centre. Avoid the horrendous taxi queue by walking a block in any direction and hailing one from the road. (www.deiracitycentre .com; Al-Garhoud Rd; ⏱10am-10pm Sun-Wed, 10am-midnight Thu-Sat)

Carrefour   SUPERMARKET

Perpetually crowded Carrefour, the city's cheapest supermarket, located at Deira City Centre (see **16** 🔒 Map p26, C8), has the best selection of international products, delicious fresh bread, Arabic pastries, Iranian caviar, cheeses from around the globe and barrels of delicious Middle Eastern olives – perfect provisions for a picnic down by the water. (Deira City Centre, Al-Garhoud Rd)

Virgin Megastore   MUSIC

Virgin's enthusiastic staff will happily suggest some souvenirs from their huge offering of Middle Eastern sounds – from oriental lounge to *khaleeji* (traditional Gulf-style music). There's also a decent selection of music, books, multimedia and electronics goods at this store in Deira City

GAVIN HELLIER/CORBIS ©

Dubai Creek (p30)

Centre (see **16** 🔒 Map p26, C8). (Deira City Centre, Al-Garhoud Rd)

Ajmal   BEAUTY

The place to buy traditional Arabic perfumes, Ajmal is always crowded with local women in elegant burkas who love to stop by the Deira City Centre (see **16** 🔒 Map p26, C8) to stock up on jewel-encrusted bottles of exotic oils. (Deira City Centre, Al-Garhoud Rd)

Al-Jaber Gallery   ARTS & CRAFTS

It may be touristy, but this cluttered store in the Deira City Centre (see **16** 🔒 Map p26, C8) has the largest selection of souvenirs and handicrafts around. Not all are from the Middle East, but those Indian cushion covers will help complete that Asian look when you get back home, while a henna kit and *sheesha* should trigger memories of your trip to Dubai. (Deira City Centre, Al-Garhoud Rd)

Magrudy's   BOOKSHOP

The best English-language bookshop in the city, Magrudy's, at the Deira City Centre (see **16** 🔒 Map p26, C8), has glossy souvenir coffee-table books, great reads on Middle Eastern history, politics and culture, the latest fiction, and a terrific travel section. (For magazines, though, head to Carrefour.) (Deira City Centre, Al-Garhoud Rd)

Mikyajy   BEAUTY

This Gulf brand's enormous local popularity is due to its vibrant col-

A classic Middle Eastern mezze plate

ours; they're made for Middle Eastern skin tones, but the vivid cosmetics brighten up any face. Stop by the outlet at Deira City Centre (see **16** 🔒 Map p26, C8) to buy the '22K' kit before hitting the clubs in Dubai. (Deira City Centre, Al-Garhoud Rd)

Lush   BEAUTY

This is more than just another natural soap and cosmetics shop, with all kinds of organic body-beautiful products: lip balms made with natural oils, foot lotion with ginger oil and cloves, lemon cuticle butter, coconut deodorant, vanilla puff talc and some wonderful perfumes (have a squirt of the orange blossom). Located at the Deira City Centre (see **16** 🔒 Map p26, C8). (Deira City Centre, Al-Garhoud Rd)

Explore

Bur Dubai

Bustling Bur Dubai is home to the superb Dubai Museum, as well as the evocative historical quarters of Bastakia and Shindagha. The Bur Dubai Souq is as lively as the Deira souqs, with the aesthetic bonus of wooden arcades and a waterfront location. The surrounding 'Little India' is lively and vibrant and the place for haggling for bargains and sipping sugary tea.

The Sights in a Day

☼ Head to lovely Bastakia for coffee and cake at cosy **XVA** (p49), then check out the exhibitions at the adjacent **Majlis Gallery** (p46). Continue to the **Bur Dubai Souq** (p44) via the striking multidomed Grand Mosque and colourful **Hindi Lane** (p44). After some browsing and bartering, enjoy lunch overlooking the bobbing boats at **Bait Al Wakeel** (p48).

☼ After lunch, backtrack to the **Dubai Museum** (pictured left; p40) for a couple of absorbing hours gleaning something of Dubai's past. Duck into **Mumtaz Mahal** (p50), the ground-floor cafe of the ornate Arabian Courtyard Hotel & Spa, for a revitalising coffee. Explore the surrounding small shops and, when it's cooler, head for the Shindagha Heritage Area beside the Creek. Don't miss the handsomely restored **Traditional Architecture Museum** (p46) or the similarly historic **Sheikh Saeed al-Maktoum House** (p46).

☽ The end of the Creekside walkway is one of Dubai's best spots for sunset views. Enjoy an avocado smoothie at **Kan Zaman** (p49) restaurant here, followed by delicious Lebanese cuisine. If you're slipping into cocktail mode, take a taxi to **Wafi Mall** (p54) for a dynamic choice of nightclubs and bars.

◉ Top Sights
Dubai Museum (p40)

♥ Best of Dubai

Eating
Asha's (p48)

Fire & Ice (p48)

Drinking
Chi (p52)

People by Crystal (p52)

Shopping
BurJuman Centre (p54)

Bateel (p55)

Getting There

Ⓜ **Metro** The metro has limited coverage here. The most central stops are Khalid Bin al-Waleed (Red and Green Lines), Al-Fahidi (Green Line) and Al Karama (Red Line).

⚓ **Ferry** The area is also served by *abra* (water taxi) and water bus from Deira Old Souq Abra & Water Bus Station.

Top Sights
Dubai Museum

Unless some mad scientist invents a time-travel machine, this excellent museum is your ticket to exploring Dubai's history in an hour or so. Exhibits are housed in the magnificent 1799 Al-Fahidi Fort, considered the oldest building in Dubai and once the seat of government and residence of Dubai's rulers. The museum traces Dubai's astonishing development from a modest desert settlement to a global centre of commerce, finance and tourism, and provides a real insight into Dubai's past and present traditions and culture.

Map p42, E2

www.dubaitourism.ae

Al-Fahidi St

adult/child Dh3/1

8.30am-8.30pm Sat-Thu, 2.30-8.30pm Fri

Traditional Arabic life on display at the Dubai Museum

Don't Miss

Multimedia Presentation

This is a real highlight, so make sure you grab a pew and watch. The 10-minute film includes some fascinating archival footage that vividly depicts just how far Dubai has come from the 1960s to today. The movie covers each decade with a pictorial tour of achievements, progress and historical milestones. It is entertaining and informative (and just the right length).

Archaeological Section

The highlight for many will be the archaeology section, with its detailed information about the local settlements believed to have been established here from around 2000–1000 BC. Don't miss the large well-lit gallery opposite the gift shop and its displays of unearthed artefacts from numerous tombs discovered in the area. At one tomb alone (Al Soufouh), 16 ceramic vessels were found. Comprehensive explanatory panelling is in English and Arabic.

The Significance of the Sea

Take a pic of the magnificent wooden dhow near the exit and wonder at the fascinating underwater pearl-diving exhibition. Snorkelers should be particularly impressed by the fact that these divers merely wore nose clips, despite descending to impossible depths. What really brings this section to life, however, is the historical footage of the pearl divers at work.

☑ Top Tips

▸ Visit early in the morning before the tour buses roll up.

▸ Take a bottle of water: there's only one vending machine – and it's near the exit.

▸ Check out the courtyard walls, made with traditional coral and gypsum.

▸ Don't bother with a tour guide: exhibits are well explained in English.

▸ Take the kids! They'll love the sound effects, films and realistic dioramas.

▸ Avoid the pricey gift shop: head for the nearby souq instead.

✕ Take a Break

For an enjoyable light meal, snack or full-on brunch head to nearby **Basta Art Cafe** (p48).

For something a tad more exotic and substantial, head to **Mumtaz Mahal** (p50) at the Arabian Courtyard Hotel.

E

Heritage & Diving Villages

Al-Shindagha Rd

3 14

6

7

Sheikh Saeed al-Maktoum House

Traditional Architecture

Al-Ghubaiba Museum

AL-RAS

Al-Ras St

Al-Ras

Bur Dubai Souq

Al-Ghubaiba

Hindi Lane

Ali bin Abi Talib St

12 4

2

Bastakia Quarter

Al-Seef Rd

1

13

5

Majlis Gallery

25

3

9

15

16

UMM HURAIR

6

Oud Metha

SHINDAGHA

Al-Ghubaiba Rd

Al-Ghubaiba Bus Station

55C

61A

Al-Ghubaiba St

Al-Nahda St

Al-Rifah St

Al-Fahidi St

Dubai Museum (Al-Fahidi Fort)

Al-Musallah Rd

16

69D

17

Khalid bin al-Waleed Rd (Bank St)

18B

Khalid bin al-Waleed

24

10A

14A

1A

9A

7C

24B

Al-Rolla Rd

15

29

18

Al-Fahidi

7

20

9A

MANKHOOL

9A

11B

15B

17B

25B

28B

25B

21

6A

14B

15

17

19A

21

Kuwait St

BUR DUBAI

Kuwait St

8C

10C

12B

25B

29

Sheikh Khalifa bin Zayed Rd (Trade Centre Rd)

Al-Mina Rd

29

37

Al-Mankhool Rd

2B

35A

37A

AL-JAFILIYA

Al-Jafiliya

22

30C

43B

2C

2D

Al Karama

Al-Adhid Rd

7C

52

1

2A

4A

6A

8A

Al-Mankhool Rd

1

9

30A

42

36

Department of Health & Medical Services

Jumeirah Rd

D

C

B

A

1

2

3

4

Dubai Creek (Khor Dubai)

Al-Maktoum Bridge

Floating Bridge

Al-Seef R

Za'abeel Rd

24

19

18A

KARAMA

Umm Hureir Rd

26

10

OUD METHA

Dubai Healthcare City

Riyadh St

Creekside Park

Karama Park

11B

22

Rashid Hospital

12

29A

29B

20B

Za'abeel Rd

2

19

8

15

14

Oud Metha Rd

20

Al-Qataiyat Rd

26

35

37B

13A

4

17A

23

10

16

47C

27

9

11

Al-Adhid Rd

Al-Wasl Hospital

Za'abeel Park

8

Sheikh Zayed Rd

ZA'ABEEL

0   500 m
0   0.25 miles

For reviews see
- Top Sights   p40
- Sights   p44
- Eating   p47
- Drinking   p52
- Entertainment   p53
- Shopping   p54

Al Jafiliya

Sights

Bastakia Quarter   HISTORIC QUARTER

1 ⊙ Map p42, E2

With its labyrinthine lanes lined with traditional wind-tower architecture, the old Bastakia Quarter on the waterfront east of Bur Dubai Souq is a magical place to explore. There are a handful of galleries and craft shops here, as well as the admirable Mawaheb from Beautiful People (www.mawaheb-dubai.com), an art studio for people with special needs. (btwn Bur Dubai waterfront, Al-Musallah Rd & Al-Fahidi St)

Bur Dubai Souq   MARKET

2 ⊙ Map p42, D2

Wander through this vibrant souvenir and textile souq and experience the hustle and bustle deep within its

Local Life
Bastakia Tours

The **Sheikh Mohammed Centre for Cultural Understanding** (see 1 ⊙ Map p42, E2; ☎04-353 6666; www.culture.ae; Bastakia), near Al-Seef Roundabout, is a unique institution founded to build bridges between cultures. It conducts insightful guided tours of the Bastakia Quarter at 10am on Sunday and Thursday (reservations advised) and organises weekly breakfasts and lunches where you can taste traditional food.

wooden-latticed arcades. Fridays sees it crowded with expat workers, mainly from India and Pakistan, on their day off, bargaining for gifts to take home, getting haircuts and buying hot Indian snacks. (btwn Bur Dubai waterfront and Ali bin Abi Talib St)

Heritage & Diving Villages   MUSEUMS

3 ⊙ Map p42, E1

On the Shindagha waterfront, the Heritage and Diving Villages are intended to acquaint tourists with the region's traditional arts, customs and architecture. This is where you can nibble on piping-hot *dosas* (paper-thin lentil-flour pancakes) made by burka-clad women, pose with a falconer, hop on a camel or browse touristy stalls. (Al-Shindagha Rd; admission free; ⊙8am-10pm Sat-Thu, 8-11am & 4-10pm Fri)

Hindi Lane   STREET

4 ⊙ Map p42, E2

Two modest temples, the Hindu Shri Nathje Jayate Temple and the Sikh Gurudwara, are hidden away behind the Grand Mosque. In a tiny alley that runs between them, known as Hindi Lane, vendors sell religious paraphernalia and temple offerings – fruit baskets, flower garlands, gold-embossed holy images, sandalwood incense and packets of bindis. (off Ali bin Abi Talib St)

Understand

Ethnic Hierarchy

There has long been criticism about the rigid social, cultural and economic divides between the Emiratis (who make up around 10% of the population), Westerners on short-term work visas and those from the developing world, particularly India. At last there are signs that these boundaries are blurring, at least at some level, with Westerners encouraged to own property and increasing numbers of Indians taking up prominent posts. India is Dubai's largest trading partner: in 2010 non-oil trade between the two countries reached a record Dh183 billion, indicating that this is a trend that is set to continue.

Human Rights

The government has also attempted to address criticism about human rights. In its 2011 World Report, the international human rights organisation Human Rights Watch applauded new UAE labour regulations that curb exploitative recruiting agents who entrap foreigners with recruiting fees and false contracts. The report lauded this positive commitment, which addresses one of the country's most glaring human rights problems – the abuse of migrant construction workers. The living conditions of such labourers remain a contentious issue. Keep your eyes peeled when you are flying into the airport here and you may well spot the segregated labour camps on the outskirts of the city, surrounded by sand. Many consider the abolition of the sponsorship (*kafala*) system, which basically strips workers of any rights, to be key among needed changes. Kuwait announced plans to scrap its *kafala* system in October 2011. It remains to be seen whether the UAE will follow suit.

Arab Spring Fallout

The extraordinary revolutionary wave of demonstrations that began on 18 December 2010 has led to authorities here becoming a tad jittery about online dissent. In November 2011, the authorities blocked access to www.localnewsuae.com, a news portal that features wide-ranging articles and blog posts on local and international issues. Downloading social networking sites, like Facebook and Twitter, onto mobile devices is also still banned, although if you have these programs already loaded on your device, there should be no problem.

Majlis Gallery

GALLERY

 5 Map p42, E2

In a charming courtyard house in the historic Bastakia Quarter, the city's oldest commercial gallery (established in 1989) exhibits art and sculpture by international and local artists, along with high-quality pottery, ceramics and glass. The central courtyard has a magnificent henna tree. The gallery also offers inexpensive two-day painting and drawing workshops. (📞04-353 6233; www .themajlisgallery.com; Al-Fahidi Roundabout; admission free; ⏰9.30am-8pm Sat-Thu)

Sheikh Saeed al-Maktoum House

MUSEUM

6 Map p42, D1

This elegant 30-room courtyard house is worth a visit as much for its gorgeous architecture as for its engaging exhibits from Dubai's pre-oil days. It also has fascinating old photographs taken in the 1940s and '50s on the Creek, in the souqs and at traditional celebrations, including some striking colour photos of girls adorned for the *tawminah* (a festival to celebrate the successful recitation of the Quran). (Al-Shindagha Rd; adult/child Dh2/1; ⏰8am-8.30pm Sat-Thu, 3-9.30pm Fri)

Traditional Architecture Museum

MUSEUM

7 Map p42, D1

Another magnificent Shindagha traditional house, this one has had stints as a residence, a jail and a police station.

Today it houses a thorough exhibition on traditional Arab architecture, including an explanation of how wind towers really work and why there are different dwelling types along the coast. Most galleries feature entertaining and informative videos which the caretaker will be only too happy to start up. (Heritage Village, Al-Shindagha Rd; admission free; ⏰8am-8pm Mon-Sat, to 2.30pm Sun)

Al Serkal Cultural Foundation

GALLERY

Next to the XVA Hotel in the lovely Bastakia Quarter (see 1 Map p42; E2), this rambling building, with its

Local Life
Desert Safaris

There's nothing like experiencing the desert, and Dubai residents – locals and expats alike – frequently make an effort to get out of the city and onto the emirate's sand-swept roads. Whether it's for a drive for some camel-spotting, a weekend of camping or a few days relaxing at a dreamy resort, it's amazing how some time in the desert can clear the head.

For travellers on short trips to Dubai, an organised 4WD desert safari is the most popular way to experience the Arabian sands. There are several reliable tour companies, including long-established **Arabian Adventures** (www.arabian -adventures.com), which offers a wide range of tours and excursions.

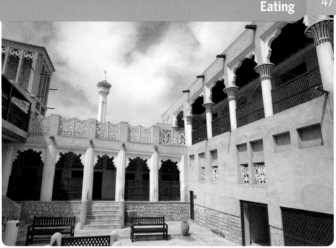

Sheikh Saeed al-Maktoum House

labyrinth of galleries set around a vast central courtyard, provides a fitting setting for both traditional and cutting-edge works by local and international artists. Exhibitions change monthly. (Al-Musallah Roundabout; admission free; ⊙9.30am-8pm Sat-Thu)

Za'abeel Park
PARK

8 ⊙ Map p42, A5

This fantastic 51-hectare park has gentle undulating green hills (perfect for picnics), gorgeous lakes and ponds, a low-impact jogging track, excellent sports facilities and kiosks – not to mention fabulous views of the Sheikh Zayed Rd skyline. It gets wonderfully packed on weekends, especially with children heading to the **Stargate** amusement park. (Sheikh Khalifa bin Zayed Rd & Al-Qataiyat Rd)

Eating

Lemongrass
THAI $$

9 ⊗ Map p42, B6

A favourite of expats, the excellent (and satisfyingly hot) traditional Thai cuisine keeps the doors swinging and the delivery guys busy. Pad Thai is presented in an omelette wrapper – a nice touch – and curries have a marvellous depth of flavour. Cool down with the house favourite *lanna* (ice cream flavoured with palm seeds, sweet corn and red beans). (near Lamcy Plaza; mains Dh35-65; ⊙noon-midnight; ⊘)

Asha's
INDIAN $$

10 🍴 Map p42, C8

Namesake of Bollywood playback singer Asha Bhosle, Asha's packs a crowd of Indian expats into its sexy, low-light, tandoori-orange dining room while dance music plays in the background. The menu focuses on contemporaryIndian fare, which translates into such palate-teasers as spicy-ginger-garlic marinated prawns and white chicken curry (with almonds, chilli seeds and yoghurt) – both Asha's personal recipes (📞04-324 4100; www.ashasrestaurants.com; Pyramids, Wafi Mall, Al-Qataiyat Rd; mains from Dh 65; ⏰12.30-3.30pm & 7.30pm-3am)

☑ Top Tip
Bargaining at the Souq
Relished by some, tedious for others, bargaining in souqs can get you a 20% to 50% discount if you're prepared to haggle. Do as the locals do: when you are offered a price, suggest 50% less. Use your gut instinct to respond to the trader's reaction, adjust your offer accordingly and then, as the process draws to an end, ask for their final and best price. If they agree to your offer, pay up. Offering a lower figure or worse yet, leaving, may be considered extremely impolite. Bargaining in a mall is acceptable if you are in carpet, computer and electronics stores.

Fire & Ice
INTERNATIONAL $$$

11 🍴 Map p42, C8

Located in the Raffles Hotel, near Wafi Mall, this modern Mediterranean-themed restaurant has terracotta brick floors and walls. Watch the chefs play with fire and ice in the open kitchen to compose hot-cold, sweet-sour taste sensations. Steaks are the specialty (order the Wagyu beef from Japan), but the seafood is just as good. The wine list is endless, with more than 400 international wines to tempt you. (📞04-314 8888; www.raffles.com; Raffles Hotel, Sheikh Rashid Rd; mains Dh95-190; ⏰dinner)

Bait Al Wakeel
MIDDLE EASTERN $

12 🍴 Map p42, E2

One of the city's most romantic settings overlooking the Creek with its view of bobbing boats, this little bit of Venice has lots of history. The building, formerly a shipping office, is one of Dubai's oldest, dating back to 1935, and the dining deck was formerly a landing stage for boats. The mezze plates are good, as are the lamb, *kofta* (minced meat and spices grilled on a skewer) and seafood. Avoid the handful of Asian dishes on the menu. (Textile Souq, Bur Dubai Souq; mains Dh35-50)

Basta Art Cafe
INTERNATIONAL $

13 🍴 Map p42, E2

This leafy courtyard cafe in a traditional wind-tower building attracts a loyal local following who head here for Farah's refreshing Basta

Understand
Buying Alcohol

One of the most common questions among first-time visitors here is – can I buy alcohol? The answer is that, in part, you can. When arriving by air, non-Muslim visitors over 18 can buy certain quantities of booze in the airport duty-free shop on arrival. With the exception of 'dry' Sharjah, where alcohol and even the smoking of *sheesha* (water pipe used to smoke tobacco) are banned, you can also purchase alcohol for on-site consumption in bars and clubs that are generally attached to four- and five-star hotels.

Expat residents can acquire an alcohol licence, which entitles them to a fixed monthly limit of alcohol available from alcohol stores. The only store where you can officially buy alcohol without a licence is at the Barracuda Beach Resort in the northern emirate of Umm al-Quwain, north of Sharjah, about an hour's drive from Dubai. Note that you are not officially allowed to transport alcohol through 'dry' Sharjah, although most people seem to take the risk.

Specials (fresh lime and mint juice) and big salads (the grilled halloumi, asparagus and mixed lettuce combo is deservedly popular). It also does delicious breakfasts and children's menus and has plenty of leafy shade. (Al-Fahidi St, Bastakia; mains Dh30-50; ⊙8am-10pm; ⦿)

XVA INTERNATIONAL $

Escape Bur Dubai's clamour and crowds at this artsy courtyard cafe in the Bastakia Quarter (see 1 ⊙ Map p42, E2). The menu eschews meat in favour of such offerings as aubergine burger, tuna salad and a vegetarian *croque monsieur* (toasted sandwich). Wash it all down with a refreshing mango juice – a must-order. (XVA Hotel, Al-Musallah Roundabout; mains Dh35-60; ⊙9am-7pm Sat-Thu; ⦿)

Noble House CHINESE $$$

Marvel over the stunning skyline views from the 17th floor at the Raffles Hotel (see 11 ✕ Map p42, C8) while you sample some of the finest and most original Szechuan and Cantonese dishes in Dubai. The decor is stylish and clubby with plush high-back tasselled chairs, and the waiting staff love to show off, especially pouring sauces from up high with perfect aim into tiny glasses. Reservations recommended. (☏04-324 8888; www.raffles.com; Raffles Hotel, Sheikh Rashid Rd; mains from Dh75; ⊙7-11.30pm Tue-Sat)

Kan Zaman MIDDLE EASTERN $$

14 ✕ Map p42, E1

A trip to Heritage Village is incomplete without a visit to this Creekside favourite. During the cooler months,

Top Tip

Bacchanalian Boating

A great way to experience the exotic magic of Old Dubai is to take a dinner cruise along the Creek. Feed tummy and soul as you gently cruise past historic waterfront houses, sparkling high-rises, jutting wind towers and wooden dhows. **Bateaux Dubai** (Map p42, 2E; ☎04-399 4994; www.bateauxdubai.com; Al-Seef Rd, Bur Dubai Creek; 2½hr dinner cruises Dh350) is an excellent choice.

the sprawling outdoor area is the place to leisurely sample mezze and grills (the tangy lamb *shwarma* – meat sliced off a spit and stuffed in a pocket of pita-type bread with chopped tomatoes and garnish – is delicious), and to watch the passing parade of boats against the backdrop of historic Deira and Bur Dubai. Afterwards, relax with some apple *sheesha* – an obligatory way to end the meal. (Heritage Village, Al-Shindagha Rd; mains Dh30-70; ☺lunch)

Shiv Ganya   VEGETARIAN $

15 🍴 Map p42, D2

The daily Dh37 buffet at this vegetarian Indian restaurant should put a satisfied waddle in your step. Favourite dishes include the traditional street snack *chaat* and *paneer* (cubes of firm white cheese) with spinach or peas and lots of spices. There is plenty of heat in the dishes; cool down with a masala mint-based tea. (Al Rolla Residence, Al-Rolla Rd; Dh18-25; ☑)

Mumtaz Mahal   INDIAN $$

16 🍴 Map p42, D2

A favourite for North Indian cuisine, located across from the museum. The tandoori specialities, excellent service and in-house Indian band and dancers make for a fun night out. Any smoky-flavoured special that comes out of the clay oven is excellent, or try the lamb *dhaba masala* (chunks of lamb in a spicy curry sauce). (Arabian Courtyard Hotel, Al-Fahidi St; mains Dh65-120; ☑)

Olive Gourmet   LEBANESE $

Right across from the metro entrance, this restaurant at the BurJuman Centre (see 24 🔒 Map p42, D4) offers reliably good and relatively inexpensive Lebanese food. Take a detour from the usual hummus-and-kebab route and order *fuul medammas* (black fava beans with lemon juice, olive oil, tomatoes and garlic) or fried calamari with garlic and lemon – served by congenial fezzed-up waiters. (BurJuman Centre, cnr Khalid bin al-Waleed & Sheikh Khalifa bin Zayed Rds; mains Dh35-48; ☑)

Antique Bazaar   INDIAN $$

17 🍴 Map p42, D3

This is not just any old curry house. Resembling an exotic Mughal palace, the decor is sumptuously ornate with carved wood seats, ivory inset tables, swing chairs and richly patterned fabrics. There's a resident sitar player at lunchtime, with more of a show at dinner, which is when the place is most atmospheric. Dishes are attrac-

Bur Dubai Souq (p44)

tively presented and the most popular include a succulent *murgh tikka lababdar* (chicken in a spicy yogurt-based sauce) and *biryanis* (rice-based curries). Reservations recommended.

☑ **Top Tip**

Time For a Cuppa?

This is the ideal region in Dubai to try a steaming cup of *masala* (also called *kadak*) *chai* – a fragrant sweet tea with green cardamom, peppercorns and cinnamon that's popular even at the height of summer. Pop into any of the Indian-run cafes or bars surrounding the Bur Dubai Souq and treat yourself to a cup or two. Delicious!

(☎04-397 7444; Four Points Sheraton, Khalid bin al-Waleed Rd; mains Dh40-50)

Wafi Gourmet   MIDDLE EASTERN $

The best deli at Wafi Mall (see **23** 🅐 Map p42, C8) has glass counters displaying delicious Arabian delicacies such as juicy olives, pickles, peppers, cheeses, freshly made hummus, *muttabal* (purée of aubergine mixed with tahini, yogurt and olive oil), tabouli and great Lebanese pastries. During the cooler months, call in here, make up a mezze plate and head down to the Creek to join the local families picnicking. (Wafi Mall, Al-Qataiyat Rd, near Al-Garhoud Bridge; light meals Dh35-60; ⏱9am-midnight)

Paul
FRENCH $

This French cafe is an upscale mall staple packed with Western expats here for the scrumptious (especially almond) croissants, ample-sized breakfasts and the small, but selective, choice of salads, sandwiches and mains. Located at the BurJuman Centre (see **24** 🔒 Map p42, D4), there are additional branches at several other malls. (BurJuman Centre; sandwiches & salads Dh35-55, mains Dh70; ⏱10am-10pm)

Lebanese Village Restaurant
LEBANESE $

18 ✖ Map p42, D3

Everything is very fresh at this Lebanese restaurant, despite the menu being so lengthy it reads like a book. There are 17 different salads for a start, including a succulent tabouli. Sit under a shady umbrella on the streetside terrace, which is more appealing than the bright diner-style interior. (Al-Mankhool Rd; mains Dh30-65; ✍)

Drinking

Chi
CLUB

19 🚇 Map p42, C6

This vast four-room venue with a Balinese-themed outdoor dance-garden is hugely popular on Dubai's clubbing circuit, particularly among young expats. There are regular theme nights (yes, dress the part), world-class DJs, and VIP cabanas.

Occasional live music; cover charge varies. (www.chinightclubdubai.com; Al-Nasr Leisureland, Oud Metha)

People by Crystal
COCKTAIL BAR

Just across the way from Fire & Ice (see **11** ✖ Map p42, C8), near Wafi Mall, this is another of the see-and-be-seen breed of sophisticated nightclub, with stylish decor, sultry lighting, excellent DJs and incredible views from the top of Raffles famous pyramid. A very special place – you *will* be back. (www.dubai.raffles.com; Raffles Hotel, Sheikh Rashid Rd; ⏱10pm-3am)

Old Vic
PUB

20 🚇 Map p42, C3

This is about as authentic as English-style pubs get in Dubai. It becomes packed with homesick Brits, here for the big-screen sports and ale on tap. The added perk is the nightly live entertainment, generally jazz, which adds a soupçon of sophistication to the place. (www.ramadadubai.com; Ramada Hotel, Al-Mankhool Rd; ⏱noon-1am)

Submarine
BAR

21 🚇 Map p42, C3

Dive into the basement of this ho-hum hotel to arrive at a compact, industrial bar popular with a refreshingly unpretentious crowd. There's often a band to kick things into gear, along with DJs that shower beat junkies with a heady mix of music, from deep house to trance, funk and R&B. Casual dress is just fine. (Dhow Palace Hotel, Al-Mankhool Rd; ⏱6pm-3am)

Entertainment

Pharaohs Club   GYM

This is the closest you'll find to an Los Angeles–style club. Located at Wafi Mall (see **23** 🅰 Map p42, C8), it has some serious weightlifting equipment (including 100lb dumbbells) for juiced-up grunters, a superb climbing wall (the highest in the region, at a dizzying 13.5m) and various fitness classes. The best amenity is the enormous, free-form 'lazy-river' rooftop swimming pool, which is available for one-day drop-ins and is great for kids. (www.wafi.com; Wafi Mall, Al-Qataiyat Rd; pool/gym use per day Dh130/200; 👬)

Wonder Bus Tours   BOAT TOUR

Twice a day (times depend on the tide), an amphibious bus, based at the BurJuman Centre (see **24** 🅰 Map p42, D4), drives down to the Creek, plunges into the water, cruises for an hour and then drives back onto land and returns to the shopping centre. (☎04-359 5656; www.wonderbustours.net; BurJuman Centre, cnr Khalid bin al-Waleed & Sheikh Khalifa bin Zayed Rds; tours adult/child Dh140/95; 👬)

Al-Nasr Leisureland   ICE SKATING

22 ⭐ Map p42, C6

Open since 1979, Leisureland is definitely long in the tooth, but it's got a bit of character and lots of facilities under one roof, including a gym, tennis and squash courts, a bowling alley and an ice rink. Sure, it's not as snazzy as the Dubai Ice Rink, but it's bigger than the one at the Hyatt Regency Dubai. Of the several eateries, Viva Goa, an Indian restaurant, is the most interesting. (www.alnasrll .com; off Oud Metha Rd, Oud Metha; adult/child Dh10/5; ⏱2hr sessions 10am, 1pm, 4pm & 7.30pm; 👬)

Fitness First   GYM

This huge global chain with a branch at the BurJuman Centre (see **24** 🅰 Map p42, D4) has state-of-the-art cardio equipment, a great line-up of classes – from body pump and spinning to Pilates and kickboxing – and a full complement of free weights. On-site trainers help you tone your muscles. (www.fitnessfirstme.com; BurJuman Centre; day pass Dh100; ⏱6am-11pm)

Understand
Saving Face in Dubai

Dubai does a roaring trade in plastic surgery, rivalling surface-deep Los Angeles for rhinoplasty, liposuction and breast augmentation. Think about it: geographically, Dubai is halfway between London and Singapore, and most of the world's airlines fly here. And all that high-end shopping means 'patients' can also build new wardrobes to match their new noses, with zero fear of running into anyone they know.

Shopping

Wafi Mall

MALL

23 🔒 Map p42, C8

With its Egyptian theme, stunning stained-glass pyramids and designer boutiques, Wafi Mall is show-stopping. The Pharaohs Club and Raffles Hotel form part of the Wafi Mall complex, ensuring there is no end to the royal pampering. Don't miss the stunning Arabian-style **Khan Murjan Souq**, accessed down the stairs by the main entrance. The mall is near Al-Garhoud Bridge. (www.waficity.com; Al-Qataiyat Rd; ⏰10am-10pm Sat-Wed, to midnight Thu & Fri)

BurJuman Centre

MALL

24 🔒 Map p42, D4

BurJuman has one of the highest concentrations of high-end labels and an easy-to-navigate floor plan with wide expanses of shiny marble studded with white leather sofas to rest weary feet. Before Dubai Mall opened, BurJuman was Dubai's most glamorous mall, with its swanky Saks Fifth Avenue, exclusive boutiques, elegant jewellery stores and French cafes. (www.burjuman.com; cnr Khalid bin al-Waleed & Sheikh Khalifa bin Zayed Rds; ⏰10am-10pm Sat-Wed, to 11pm Thu & Fri)

MOODBOARD/CORBIS ©

Curly-toed slippers for sale

☑ Top Tip

A Great Gift

The de rigueur gift for any proper gourmet, Bateel dates are the ultimate luxury food of Arabia. At first glance, Bateel looks like a jewellery store, with polished glass display cases and halogen pin spots illuminating the goods. A closer look reveals perfectly aligned pyramids of dates – thousands of them. Bateel plays to its audience with gorgeous packaging that might leave the recipient of your gift expecting gold or silver within. The dates come from Saudi Arabia, which has the ideal growing conditions: sandy, alkaline soil and extreme heat. Quality control is tight: Bateel has its own farms and production equipment. The dates sold here are big and fat, with gooey-moist centres.

Bateel
FOOD

Bateel is located at several of Dubai's shopping malls, including the BurJuman Centre (see **24** 🔒 Map p42, D4). European chocolate-making techniques are applied to quality local dates to produce the most delicious date chocolates, truffles, marzipan and nougat, along with date jams and a sparkling date drink. (www.bateel.com; BurJuman Centre, cnr Khalid bin al-Waleed & Sheikh Khalifa bin Zayed Rds)

Allah Din Shoes
SOUVENIRS

This small outdoor stall near the *abra* dock in Bur Dubai Souq (see **2** ◉ Map p42, D2) was the first to offer fabulous sequinned slippers and gold-thread curly-toed shoes from Pakistan and Afghanistan. Although everyone's selling them now, it's still the best for quality and variety. (abra dock; ⊘10am-10pm Sat-Thu, 4-10pm Fri)

Al-Orooba Oriental
SOUVENIRS

Located at the BurJuman Centre (see **24** 🔒 Map p42, D4), this is one of Dubai's few stores to stock authentic antiques and quality collectables. It has an impressive selection of Bedouin jewellery, old *khanjars* (traditional curved daggers), beautiful ceramics and miniature Persian paintings and carpets. (BurJuman Centre, cnr Khalid bin al-Waleed & Sheikh Khalifa bin Zayed Rds)

Shoppers Department Store
DEPARTMENT STORE

25 🔒 Map p42, E3

Head upstairs in this Pakistani-run department store for a fine array of colourful and traditional Punjabi tunic tops, which look great with jeans or leggings and start at just Dh50. The mega-bling babywear for girls is also pretty eye-catching, with enough taffeta and frills to blow their little socks off. Located just east of the Al-Fahidi roundabout. (Al-Musallah Rd)

☑ Top Tip

Tailor-Made Fashion

The backstreets of Bur Dubai are filled with talented Indian tailors who will knock off a perfect copy of your favourite dress or suit in a couple of days. Some sell material as well, although you would be better off visiting the nearby Textile Souq (within the main Bur Dubai Souq), where you can ponder over endless swatches of wonderful fabrics. The best tailoring street is Al-Hisn St (off Al-Fahidi St, near Dubai Museum), where reliable tailors include the poetically named **Dream Girls** and **Hollywood Tailors**. Expect to pay around Dh150 for a dress and allow at least three days for getting your garment sewn up.

Ajmal   PERFUME

The place at the BurJuman Centre (see 24 🔒 Map p42, D4) for traditional Arabian *attars* (perfumes) and essential oils, Ajmal custom-blends its earthy scents and pours them into fancy gold or jewel-encrusted bottles. These aren't fancy French colognes – they're woody and pungent perfumes. Ask for the signature scent 'Ajmal', based on white musk and jasmine (Dh300). Other branches are in Deira City Centre, Mall of the Emirates and Dubai Mall. (www.ajmalperfume.com; BurJuman Centre, cnr Khalid bin al-Waleed & Sheikh Khalifa bin Zayed Rds)

Five Green   FASHION

26 🔒 Map p42, D6

This edgy boutique and art space owned by siblings Shahi and Shehab Hamad sells unisex urban streetwear from Paul Frank, GSUS, XLarge and BoxFresh, along with Dubai-based designers Saadia Zahid and Mona Ibrahim. Here you will also come across idiosyncratic shoes and Lomo cameras, as well as indie mags and music. Check out the vinyl art collectibles. (Aroma Garden Café Bldg, Oud Metha; ☺10am-11pm Sat-Thu, 4-11pm Fri)

Karama Shopping Centre   ARTS, CRAFTS & SOUVENIRS

27 🔒 Map p42, B5

Savvy shoppers and lovers of kitsch (Burj al-Arab paperweight, anyone?) save their souvenir shopping for Karama. It's cheaper than the malls, and those keen on under-the-counter designer fakes will welcome the repetitive call of 'copy watches, copy bags, madam'. (18B St, btwn 33B & 45B Sts)

Gift World   ARTS & CRAFTS

There's little space to move in this wonderfully cluttered Aladdin's Cave at the Karama Shopping Centre (see 27 🔒 Map p42, B5). You'll bump your head on Moroccan lanterns and Syrian hanging lamps as you rummage through the oriental bric-a-brac for that unique piece of Bedouin jewellery or search stacks of sequined bedspreads for that perfect colour. (Block T, Karama Shopping Centre, 18B St, btwn 33B & 45B Sts; ☺9am-10.30pm Sat-Thu, 4-10.30pm Fri)

IMAANIIOOO/DREAMSTIME.COM ©

Perfume bottles on display

Top Tip

Perfume Shopping

Shopping for perfume can wear out your sense of smell. If you're in the market for Arabian scents, do what top perfumers do to neutralise their olfactory palate: close your mouth and make three forceful exhalations through your nose. Blast the air hard, in short bursts, using your diaphragm. Blowing your nose first is probably a wise idea... Some people incorrectly say to smell coffee grounds, but this just numbs your sense of smell.

Royal Saffron   SPICES

Royal Saffron is easy to find, just around the corner from the Majlis Gallery (see 5 Map p42, E2), or just follow the wafting smell of burning *bakhoor* (incense tablets). The spice souq is condensed into this one tiny shop, which has fresh spices like cloves, cardamom and cinnamon, fragrant oils, dried fruits and nuts, frankincense from Somalia and Oman, henna hair dye – and quirky salt and pepper sheikh and sheikhas. (Bastakia Quarter)

Explore

Jumeirah Downtown

The northeast or downtown area of Jumeirah is full of contrasts and is a fascinating neighbourhood to explore. The chief sights vary from great sandy stretches to the densely populated district of Satwa, with its earthy souq-like ambience and candy-coloured houses. Some of the best ethnic restaurants can be found here as well, plus the city's magnificent main mosque.

The Sights in a Day

☀ Cruise into your day with an early-morning stroll on the sand at the **Jumeirah Open Beach** (p62). Next, aim for a perfect balance of spirituality and architecture at the **Jumeirah Mosque** (pictured left; p62), before feeding the body with some healthy soul food over a late-morning brunch at the **Lime Tree Cafe** (p62).

☀ Continue in culture mode by enjoying fine artwork at the **Pro Art Gallery** (p62), then indulge, big time, with a shopping spree at original local boutiques like **S*uce** (p64) and **Blue Cactus** (p65). Enjoy a late lunch with a legendary Pakistani curry at **Ravi** (p62).

☾ Take a pleasurable walk down the lively Satwa thoroughfare of Al-Dhiyafah. Head back to the beach in time for sunset, before shifting into Latino mode at **Malecon** (p64) with Cuban food followed by a few salsa twirls on the dance floor.

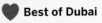 Best of Dubai

Eating
Ravi (p62)

Lime Tree Cafe (p62)

Drinking
Malecon (p64)

Boutique Shopping
S*uce (p64)

Blue Cactus (p65)

Getting There

Ⓜ **Metro** There is really no convenient metro stop for the Jumeirah Open Beach area, so a taxi is recommended. Most hotels in the area also operate regular shuttle buses to the beaches. The nearest metro stops (Red Line) for Satwa are Al-Jafiliya and the World Trade Centre, but both will require a short additional taxi ride (approximately Dh10).

A **B** **C** **D**

0   500 m
0   0.25 miles

1

Arabian Gulf

Jumeirah
Beach
Park

2

2

14D

75B

🔒
13

79

71B

26C
28B

32C

65B

69B

2D

Al-Wasl Rd

JUMEIRAH 2

13th St

Al-Safa St

3

Umm Amara St

4

13th St

58A

Business
Bay
Ⓜ

*Interchange
No 1*

Ⓜ
**Burj Khalifa/
Dubai Mall**

Financial Centre Rd

5

For reviews see
⊙ Sights	p62
⊗ Eating	p62
🍷 Drinking	p64
🔒 Shopping	p64

**DOWNTOWN
DUBAI**

E   F   G   H

1

Jumeirah Open Beach ◉4

3◉ Pro Art Gallery

♀ 10

11 🔒

5 3

Jumeirah Mosque

2A

Jumeirah Rd

12 🔒

15B 11

27B

⊗ 9 1◉

6B

8A
14A

6D

43A 35A

6C

10C

24B

5 3 24A

2A 7A

45A 41A

16C

39B

16B

33

24C

21A

17B

2A

6A

8A

9

12A

3C

8
⊗

590

15

20B

24D

2B

21B

31

27A

2A

JUMEIRAH 1

6B

23

21

12B

8B

17B

5
⊗

2C

49

45

41

20B

63

75

Al-Satwa Rd

Al-Satwa Rd

6B

10B

8A

19

17

13A

6A

12A

7
⊗

3

57A

SATWA

18B

20B

20A

22A

22B

30A

11

Al-Dhiyafah Rd

32C

308

83B

73B

57

15

11

World Trade Centre Ⓜ

Za'abeel Roundabout (World Trade Centre Roundabout)

4

308

19

Sheikh Zayed Rd Ⓜ

2

37

Emirates Tower

Ⓜ

Financial Centre

7

21

17

FINANCIAL DISTRICT

312

Horse Racecourse

2nd Za'abeel Rd

5

Sights

Jumeirah Mosque
MOSQUE

1 ⦿ Map p60, G2

This splendid mosque is a sight to behold when it is stunningly lit at night. It can only be visited inside on a guided tour, which wraps up with a Q&A session. There's no need to pre-book; just register at the mosque before the tour. Put it at the top of your to-do list, turn up early and dress modestly. (Jumeirah Rd; admission free; ☺tours 10am Tue, Thu, Sat & Sun)

Jumeirah Beach Park
BEACH

2 ⦿ Map p60, A2

With its shady palm trees, manicured lawns and long stretch of beach, Dubai's favourite park gets packed on weekends. Facilities are excellent, with a children's playground, barbecues, picnic tables and kiosks, as well as lifeguards on duty. (Jumeirah Rd; per person/car Dh5/20; ☺8am-10.30pm, women & children only Sat)

Pro Art Gallery
GALLERY

3 ⦿ Map p60, F1

Based on an extraordinary donated private collection, this gallery is more like an art museum with original paintings, lithographs and sculptures by such masters as Chagall, Dufy, Damien Hirst, Arman, Le Corbusier (yes, he was an artist too!) and Picasso. These days the gallery concentrates on street art – there are a couple of original works by Banksy here – with a vibrant program of regular exhibitions. (www.proartuae.com; Palm Strip Mall, Jumeirah Rd; ☺10am-10pm Sat-Thu)

Jumeirah Open Beach
BEACH

4 ⦿ Map p60, F1

Also known as Russian Beach because of its popularity with Russian tourists, this stretch of white sand gets crowded with a mix of sun-worshipping tourists and resident expats. It's a pleasant beach with showers and a kiosk (where you can also rent sunbeds and umbrellas). There are good eating and drinking options at the adjacent Dubai Marine Beach Resort & Spa. (next to Dubai Marine Beach Resort & Spa)

Eating

Ravi
PAKISTANI $

5 🍴 Map p60, H3

Best known for its cheap prices, long opening hours and street-savvy outdoor seating, Ravi is a Dubai institution. The meat dishes are reliably good and there is plenty of vegetarian choice, including a tasty *biryani* (curry with rice). Wash your meal down with a sweet lassi, then watch Satwa's passing parade. (Al-Satwa Rd, Satwa; mains Dh15-20; ☺24hr; 🖉)

Lime Tree Cafe
CAFE $

6 🍴 Map p60, G2

This lime-green villa is in a state of perpetual 'coffee morning' – and lingering breakfasts over the weekend

Understand
Lebanese Food Lingo 101

Break the hummus habit and try something new. Here's a primer to help you navigate some lesser-known dishes on Dubai's ubiquitous Lebanese menus. (Spellings may vary.)

Fattoosh Chopped salad topped with fried Lebanese bread and a dressing of olive oil, lemon and sumac.

Kibbeh Balls of minced lamb and onion, rolled in cracked wheat and fried.

Kibbeh nayye Ground raw lamb served with egg and condiments.

Kofta Grilled skewers of spicy minced lamb.

Labneh Thick, strained yogurt that's spreadable like cream cheese.

Muhammara Paste of red capsicum, nuts, breadcrumbs and pomegranate.

Sambusak Pastries stuffed with ground lamb or cheese.

Shish tawooq Spiced chunks of chargrilled chicken.

Shwarma Rotisserie-cooked seasoned lamb or chicken, carved onto flat-bread and rolled up with salad and sauce.

papers. The original Western expat-style cafe to hit Dubai, it's still one of the best. Great salads and superlative carrot cake. There's a newer second branch in Al-Quoz. (Jumeirah Rd; mains Dh20-40; ☺7.30am-6pm; ⚡🚼)

Pars Iranian Kitchen
IRANIAN $

7 🍴 Map p60, H3

Enjoy hot wheels of bread made daily in the outside brick oven along with such classics as creamy *muttabal* (purée of aubergine mixed with tahini, lemon and olive oil), hummus and juicy Iranian-style spicy kebabs paired with buttery saffron rice. You'll feel like royalty lounging amid the fat pillows on a carpeted platform surrounded by twinkle-lit hedges. (Satwa Roundabout, Satwa; mains Dh35-55; ☺6pm-1am; 🚼)

Al Mallah
LEBANESE $$

8 🍴 Map p60, H2

Neon-lit Al Mallah is a local favourite, seeing waves of customers converge on its outdoor terrace, even when the thermometer is about to burst in summer. While all the Lebanese dishes on offer are excellent, most people come for the great *shwarmas* and fresh juices. (Al-Dhiyafah Rd, Satwa; mains Dh50-75; ☺6am-4am)

Japengo Cafe
INTERNATIONAL $

Grab a window or terrace seat for great views of the Jumeirah Mosque. Decorated with plenty of rattan contrasting with shiny black, the menu is vast and varied, featuring dishes from East to West. Opt for the East or, more specifically, the Indonesian-style *nasi goreng istimewa* (fried rice with sausages, eggs and prawns), sushi, sashimi, tempura or a delicately spiced curry. Located just below the Pro Art Gallery (see 3 ◉ Map p60, F1). (Palm Strip Mall, Jumeirah Rd; mains Dh30-50; 🏠)

THE One
CAFE $

9 ✕ Map p60, G2

Deli dabblers will be in salad and sandwich heaven at this stylish outpost upstairs at THE One home design store. All food is freshly prepared and calibrated to health and waist watchers without sacrificing taste. Reliable choices include the smoked salmon wrap and the traditional chicken salad. A good alternative if Lime Tree Cafe is full. (Jumeirah Rd, Jumeirah 1; mains Dh35-70; ⏱9am-9pm)

Drinking

Malecon
BAR

10 🍺 Map p60, G1

Tequila is the essential drink at Malecon, an important stopover for the party crowd after 10pm or so (come earlier for tasty Cuban food). This Latino-inspired bar is the

☑️ Top Tip

Shwarma Time

Wander down lively Al-Dhiyafah Rd in Satwa, stopping for a snack at one of the earthy cheap-eat restaurants or cafes. Lit up in brilliant neon splendour, **Al Mallah** is a popular choice, especially for the lamb and chicken *shwarmas* and felafel sandwiches. This is one of the most atmospheric and bustling streets in the city, with crowds of people and a wide pavement – a rarity in Dubai!

place to hit late, do shots and twirl with a Cuban heel. Look sharp. (www.dxbmarine.com; Dubai Marine Beach Resort & Spa, Jumeirah Rd; ⏱7pm-3am)

Boudoir
BAR

Red velvet booths, hanging glass beads and crystal chandeliers make baroque Boudoir one of Dubai's most glamorous bars. It's in the same resort as Malecon (see 10 🍺 Map p60, G1). Starting the night in style as a restaurant-cum-cocktail bar, it becomes a decadent dance club when the clock strikes 12. (www.dxbmarine.com; Dubai Marine Beach Resort & Spa, Jumeirah Rd; ⏱7.30pm-3am)

Shopping

S*uce
FASHION

11 🔒 Map p60, F1

One of only a few truly independent boutiques in Dubai, run by three funky fashionistas, this chic store stocks idiosyncratic women's labels including Sass & Bide, Tata-Naka and Tsumori Chisato. This is also the place to grab sassy accessories and jewellery, as well as very feminine home and design objects. (The Village Mall, Jumeirah Rd; ⏱10am-10pm Sat-Thu, 4.30-10pm Fri)

Blue Cactus   FASHION

12 🔒 Map p60, F2

The buyer at this upstairs boutique is from Mexico, hence the Frida Kahlo emphasis in the decor and brilliant colours and patterns in the fashions and accessories. There are sleek long dresses, sassy separates and some seriously Ascot-worthy hats, as well as a cool collection of Mexican silver jewellery. (Jumeirah Centre, Jumeirah Rd)

Fleurt   FASHION

This small boutique at the Mercato Mall (see 13 🔒 Map p60, D2) keeps trend-hungry stylistas looking good in funky-smart fashions by Betsey Johnson and Soul Revival, among other progressives. The collection is refreshingly offbeat, with sequins, curve-hugging lines and cheeky party frocks. (Mercato Mall, Jumeirah Rd; ⏱10am-10pm Sat-Thu, 1.30-10pm Fri)

Mercato Mall   SHOPPING MALL

13 🔒 Map p60, D2

The Florentine-cum-Venetian architecture, glass ceilings, murals of Venice and mazes of *calle* (little lanes) is kitsch, but charmingly so. You'll find the usual range of brands like Bersh-

ka, Mango and Promod, along with shoes, cosmetics, accessories, cinemas and cafes – well positioned for observing the passing crowds. (Jumeirah Rd; ⏱10am-10pm Sat-Thu, 2-10pm Fri)

Persian Carpet House & Antiques   ARTS & CRAFTS

The outstanding Persian Carpet House at Mercato Mall (see 13 🔒 Map p60, D2) stocks a wide variety of exquisite handwoven carpets from Iran, India, Kashmir, Pakistan and Afghanistan, as well as a smaller range from Turkey, China and Russia, along with oriental antiques and curios. (Mercato Mall, Jumeirah Rd; ⏱10am-10pm Thu-Sat, 2-10pm Fri)

JEAN-PIERRE LESCOURRET/LONELY PLANET IMAGES ©

Mercato Mall, developed by Al Zarooni Group

Explore

Madinat Jumeirah & Around

This beautiful stretch of coast boasts some top beach resorts, plus boutique shopping, copious spas and health clubs, and a mix of BMWs and expensive 4WDs in villa driveways. Jumeirah is also home to Dubai's most iconic hotel – the Burj al-Arab – and a stunning Little Venice–style development. Night owls will find plenty of scope for stargazing while sipping cocktails at celeb-studded clubs.

The Sights in a Day

☀️ Enjoy some green space at the large and leafy **Safa Park** (p77). Have a sandwich snack at one of the kiosks here, then feed any crumbs left to the ducks. It's a short journey to the beautifully restored **Majlis Ghorfat Um-al-Sheef** (p72), a traditional Arab house. Enjoy a good look around then move on to do a little boutique shopping on the beach road.

☀️ It's late lunchtime by now, so head straight to **Madinat Jumeirah** (p68), where there are plenty of superb restaurants. Next up, check out the souq-style shops, camera-click the iconic **Burj al-Arab** (pictured left; p72) and consider cooling down big-time at the **Wild Wadi Waterpark** (p76).

🌙 Join the khaki-clad tourists and expats for a pre-dinner drink at **The Agency** (p74) before snagging a romantic outside table at the spectacular **Zheng He's** (p72). Top off the evening in brave traditional style by swinging by the **Bahri Bar** (p74) for a camel-milk-cocktail nightcap (sure beats a cup of cocoa).

👁 Top Sights
Madinat Jumeirah (p68)

❤️ Best of Dubai

Eating
The Meat Company (p72)

Drinking
360° (p74)

Bahri Bar (p74)

Beaches
Kite Beach (p72)

Umm Suqeim Beach (p72)

Getting There

Ⓜ **Metro** The closest metro stop to Madinat Jumeirah is Mall of the Emirates (Red Line). Although the metro stop is some distance from this area, there are regular feeder buses that meet the metro. Alternatively you can take a taxi for the 2km trip (Dh10).

Top Sights
Madinat Jumeirah

A city within a city, the Madinat Jumeirah is a Dubai must-see. There's plenty to do at this fanciful hotel, shopping and entertainment complex that has the Burj al-Arab in the background. Explore the Arabian-style architecture, snoop around the splendid Al-Qasr and Mina A'Salam hotels or get lost in the labyrinth of the souvenir-saturated souq. There are some exquisite details throughout, so if you see some stairs, take them: they might lead you to a secret terrace with a mesmerising vista of the sprawling complex.

Map p70, A3

www.dubaitourism.ae

Al-Sufouh Rd, Umm Suqeim 3

M Mall of the Emirates (Red Line)

Al-Qasr hotel and canal

Don't Miss

Abra Cruising

If you're a hotel guest, or have a restaurant reservation, you can *abra*-cruise along the 4km-long network of Venetian-style canals for free. Otherwise it costs Dh50, but it's well worth it. The desert will seem a long way away as your traditional wooden boat glides past scrupulously maintained gardens of billowing bougainvillea, bushy banana trees and soaring palms, all set against the dramatic Burj al-Arab backdrop.

Tea at the Burj

This is one afternoon tea that's definitely a brew above the others. It's not cheap – expect to pay between Dh275 and Dh425 – but for pure novelty value it's a winner. There are several afternoon-tea styles available (including Asian) aside from the traditional English variety (with scones and the best china cups, naturally). Alternatively, come for cocktails (8pm to 1am), accompanied by live jazz. Reservations essential.

Hotel Snooping

Even if you are not staying at Madinat's Al-Qasr or Mina A'Salam hotels, at least dip into them to have a look at the magnificent Arabian-style architecture and have a coffee, drink or meal at one of the stunning restaurants. The detail of the decor, artwork and furnishings is exotically palatial. If you can stay here, even better...

☑ Top Tips

▶ If you are staying in a hotel here, or eating at one of the restaurants, your *abra* trip is free.

▶ Advance reservations are essential at Madinat Jumeirah's restaurants.

▶ Book a night at the local theatre here – a rare treat in Dubai.

▶ Maps are available at several information points.

✕ Take a Break

Enjoy a long cold drink or cocktail at the **Left Bank** (p75), a welcoming bar overlooking the picturesque canals. Or go for something more substantial with a delicious seafood dinner at chic and sophisticated **Pierchic** (p74), with its gorgeous vistas of the Burj al-Arab and the Madinat Jumeirah souq.

A   B   C   D

1

Arabian Gulf

2

1 ◉ *Burj al-Arab*

◉ 5

Umm Suqeim Beach

◎ 3

Kite Beac

◉ 2

Madinat Jumeirah ◉

✪ 6

Jumeirah Beach Rd

UMM SUQEIM 2

🔒 8

Al-Sufouh Rd

3

Umm Suqeim Rd

UMM SUQEIM 3

Al-Wasl Rd

4

Interchange No 4

Ⓜ **Mall of the Emirates**

First Gulf Bank Ⓜ

Sheikh Zayed Rd

Interchange No 3

4B St

6

8

8

Al-Rassas Rd

AL-QUOZ

18

For reviews see	
◉ Top Sights	p68
◎ Sights	p72
✕ Eating	p72
🅠 Drinking	p74
✪ Entertainment	p76
🔒 Shopping	p77

5

0 — 1 km
0 — 0.5 miles

Jumeirah Beach Rd

9

10

Umm Al-Sheif St

UMM SUQEIM 1

Al-Wasl Rd

4
Majlis Ghorfat Um-al-Sheef

JUMEIRAH 2

Attar St

JUMEIRAH 3

SAFA

Al-Hadiqa St

7

Sheikh Zayed Rd

M Al-Quoz

Interchange No 2

Meydan Rd

E F G H

1

2

3

4

5

Sights

Burj al-Arab
HOTEL

1 ⊙ Map p70, A2

Since opening in 1999, the Burj al-Arab has been a symbol of a booming city in the sand. It's built on an artificial island 280m offshore from the Jumeirah Beach Hotel, to which it is linked by a causeway. The Burj is worth visiting, if only to gawk at an interior clad in some 1600 sq metres of gold leaf. (☎04-301 7000; www.burj-al-arab.com; Jumeirah Beach Rd, Umm Suqeim 3)

Kite Beach
BEACH

2 ⊙ Map p70, D2

There's plenty of room to sunbathe comfortably on this long, pristine beach while you watch the action provided by the local kitesurfer community (hence the name), whose abilities range from good to good grief. No facilities. (Umm Suqeim 4)

Umm Suqeim Beach
BEACH

3 ⊙ Map p70, B2

Between Jumeirah Beach Hotel and Kite Beach, this white-sand beach with fabulous views of the Burj al-Arab is popular with Jumeirah families and a more body-conscious set, as well as surfers during the winter months. There are showers but little shelter, so don't forget that floppy hat and sunscreen. (next to Jumeirah Beach Hotel, Jumeirah Beach Rd)

Majlis Ghorfat Um-al-Sheef
HISTORIC BUILDING

4 ⊙ Map p70, G2

This elegant gypsum-and-coral-rock two-storey *majlis* (meeting place) was built in 1955 for former ruler Sheikh Rashid bin Saeed al-Maktoum to listen to his people's complaints, grievances and ideas. Beautifully restored and elaborately decorated, it offers an authentic snapshot of Dubai during the 1950s. (17 St, off Jumeirah Beach Rd, Jumeirah; admission Dh1; ⊙8.30am-1.30pm & 3.30-8.30pm Sat-Thu, 3.30-8.30pm Fri)

Eating

The Meat Company
STEAKHOUSE $

Overlooking the canals at Madinat Jumeirah (see ⊙ Map p70, A3) with the Burj al-Arab backdrop, this place takes its meat seriously and gives you a beefy choice, ranging from an Australian grain-fed Angus to a Brazilian grass-fed beast. Other options include a hanging skewer of marinated lamb, and there are several veggie sides like wild mushrooms. This is a popular VIP place judging by the signed plates on the wall. (☎04-368 6040; Madinat Jumeirah, Al-Sufouh Rd, Umm Suqeim 3; mains Dh85-120; ⊙dinner)

Zheng He's
CHINESE $$$

From the authentic dim sum to the inventive desserts, Zheng He's at Madinat Jumeirah (see ⊙ Map p70, A3) serves up wonderful flavours (try any of the seafood offerings) with eye-catching

Understand

The Emirati Lifestyle

Don't be surprised if you hear expats make crude generalisations about Emiratis. You may be told that they're all millionaires and live in mansions, or that they refuse to work in ordinary jobs, or that all the men have four wives. Such stereotypes simply reinforce prejudices and demonstrate the lack of understanding between cultures in Dubai.

Not all Emiratis are wealthy. While the traditional tribal leaders, or sheikhs, are often the wealthiest UAE nationals, many have made their fortune through good investments, often dating back to the 1970s. All Emiratis have access to free health care and education as well as a marriage fund (although the budgets don't often meet the expenses of elaborate Emirati weddings). These types of social benefits, and charities operated by generous sheikhs, such as Sheikh Mohammed bin Rashid al-Maktoum, are essential to the survival of poorer Emiratis in modern Dubai.

The Majlis

The upper and middle classes of Emirati society generally have expansive villas in which men and women still live apart, and where male family members entertain guests in the *majlis*. In all classes of Emirati society, extended families living together is the norm, with the woman moving in with the husband's family after marriage, although some young couples are now choosing to buy their own apartments for a little more privacy than the traditional arrangement allows.

Heritage & Tradition

Dubai has been quite active in preserving and publicly displaying many local sights and traditions that provide insights into traditional and cultural life. The aim of such preservation efforts is not just to attract and entertain tourists, but to educate young Emiratis about their culture and heritage. Families also make an effort to maintain their heritage by taking their children out to the desert frequently and teaching them how to continue traditional practices such as falconry. The love of the desert is also something that is passed from father to son – Emiratis are as comfortable in the sands as they are in Switzerland, where many of them take a summer break away from the heat.

○ Local Life
Vegetarian Restaurants
Good news: restaurants with poor vegetarian selections are the exception in Dubai. You can thank all the wonderful cooking from the Indian subcontinent, the Middle East and Thailand. The city's many Indian restaurants do fantastic things with spiced vegetables and rice. At any Lebanese restaurant, you can fill the table with the all-veg mezzes for a small feast. At Thai places, plan to eat rice dishes with vegetable coconut curries. And although you vegans out there may have to ask more questions, you shouldn't have a hard time finding something to eat here either.

presentation. The interior is dazzling, but alfresco tables have a stunning view of the Burj al-Arab (book well ahead). (☏04-366 8888; Mina A'Salam, Madinat Jumeirah, Al-Sufouh Rd, Umm Suqeim 3; mains Dh75-240)

Pierchic
SEAFOOD $$$

The stroll down the pier to this water-bound restaurant is best taken for dinner, when Madinat Jumeirah (see ⊙ Map p70, A3) twinkles onshore and the Burj al-Arab light show is mesmerising – ask for a seaside table. Dinner will damage your wallet, but if romance is on the menu, this is the perfect setting. (☏04-399 9999; Al-Qasr, Madinat Jumeirah, Al-Sufouh Rd, Umm Suqeim 3; mains Dh100-240)

Drinking

360°
BAR

5 🚇 Map p70, B2

This stunning rooftop bar with white loungers and sublime views of Burj al-Arab sees a beautiful set kicking back on Friday evenings for sundowners, especially when a good DJ is scheduled. But it's only doable in the cooler months, when the temperatures aren't rising over 40 degrees. (Jumeirah Beach Hotel, off Jumeirah Beach Rd; ◷5pm-2am)

The Agency
WINE BAR

This stylish wine bar at Madinat Jumeirah (see ⊙ Map p70, A3) is a good choice any time, with comfy low leather seats for couples who want to get cosy and high tables for the groups who like to mingle. There's an excellent list of wines by the glass and tasty tapas-size snacks – chorizo mash, spicy prawns and juicy olives. (Madinat Jumeirah, Al-Sufouh Rd, Umm Suqeim 3; ◷noon-1am)

Bahri Bar
COCKTAIL BAR

One of Dubai's most ambient bars, located in Madinat Jumeirah (see ⊙ Map p70, A3), Bahri is perfect for a sunset drink: the view of the palm-lined beach, the Madinat's meandering canals, and the Burj al-Arab is stunning. After sunset, the kaleidoscopic light show on the giant sail is breathtaking. (Madinat Jumeirah, Al-Sufouh Rd, Umm Suqeim 3; ◷noon-2am)

Bar Zar
BAR

Bar Zar is good for pre-club cocktails at Madinat Jumeirah (see  Map p70, A3). Skip the glorified sports bar upstairs and report straight to the waterfront terrace to sip cold beers and killer cosmos. There are different nightly promotions, including women's night on Monday.

Left Bank
BAR

Abras float past the waterfront terrace at this popular bar in Madinat Jumeirah (see ◉ Map p70, A3), while neon lighting, low leather lounges and chill beats draw a laid-back crowd indoors. Order a cocktail so the enthusiastic waiter can entertain you with a shaker, crushed ice and a few smooth moves. (Souq Madinat Jumeirah, Al-Sufouh Rd, Umm Suqeim 3; ⏰noon-2am)

Trilogy
CLUB

Covering three floors with Moroccan-inspired decor and a sumptuous gold-and-silver colour scheme, this is another place in Madinat Jumeirah (see ◉ Map p70, A3) that brings in the best on the international DJ circuit. It's located at the entrance to the souq so it's easy to find – thankfully, given those teetering high heels you're sporting. (Souq Madinat Jumeira, Al-Sufouh Rd, Umm Suqeim 3; ⏰9pm-late)

Madinat Jumeirah restaurant

MASSIMO BORCHI/4CORNERS ©

Understand

Sheesha: A Primer

Sheesha pipes (water pipes used to smoke tobacco) are packed with tobacco in such flavours as apple, anise, strawberry, vanilla and coffee – the range of flavours is endless. Here's a primer on how to smoke the pipe back home:

▶ Fill the glass bowl with water and fix the metal tube into it, ensuring that the tube is underwater.

▶ Next, return the metal plate to the top of the tube and place the bowl atop.

▶ Fill the bowl with some loose *sheesha* tobacco and cover tightly with foil, before poking about five holes into it with a skewer or fork.

▶ Using tongs, heat up some Magic Coal, the preferred brand of charcoal, on a stove (or hotplate) over a gas burner, then pop it on top of the foil.

▶ Lastly, place the pipe into the hole on the side of the *sheesha* pipe, pop a disposable plastic mouthpiece on the end if you're planning to share, and take a long hard puff on the pipe.

▶ Recline on the oriental cushions you bought at the souqs and remember your time in Dubai.

Entertainment

Wild Wadi Waterpark   WATER PARK

6 ⭐ Map p70, A2

There's no better way to cool down in Dubai than heading to Wild Wadi for the day. There are plenty of gentle rides for tots, plus a big-wave pool, a white-water rapids 'river' and a 33m-high Jumeirah Sceirah slide that drops you at a speed of 80km/h (hold on to your trunks, guys!). Thrillseekers can also test their bodyboarding mettle on Wipeout, a permanent wave. (☎04-348 4444; www.wildwadi.com; Jumeirah Beach Rd, Umm Suqeim 3; adult/child Dh205/165; ⏰10am-6pm Nov-Feb, to 7pm Mar-May & Sep-Oct, to 9pm June-Aug)

Jam Base   LIVE MUSIC

This stylish venue at Madinat Jumeirah (see ◉ Map p70, A3) is the place to head for live jazz, R&B and soul, as well as fresh fusion cuisine (it also offers a pre-theatre menu). The bands know how to work a crowd, and the dance floor jumps on weekends. (Souq Madinat Jumeirah, Al-Sufouh Rd, Umm Suqeim 3; ⏰7pm-2am)

Madinat Theatre
THEATRE

A regular program of crowd-pleasing entertainment from *The Sound of Music* to Russian ballet keeps Dubai's culture-starved residents happy at this local theatre at Madinat Jumeirah (see 📍 Map p70, A3). Performances may take place in the theatre, the large arena, or outdoors at the waterside amphitheatre. (☎04-366 6546/50; Souq Madinat Jumeirah, Al-Sufouh Rd, Umm Suqeim 3; tickets Dh100-300; ⏱box office 10am-10pm)

Al-Safa Park
PARK

7 ⭐ Map p70, H3

Bordered by Sheikh Zayed and Al-Wasl Rds, this pretty and popular park is a pastiche of lawn, gardens (including a ladies' garden), waterfalls, children's playgrounds and even a lake where you can feed the ducks or take your sweetie for a spin in a rowing or paddle boat. The Dubai Flea Market is held here once a month October to May. Tuesday is for women and children only. (Al-Wasl Rd & Al-Hadiqa St, Safa; admission Dh5; ⏱8am-11pm)

Shopping

Gallery One Fine Art Photographs
ART

The splendid framed photographs at this shop at Souq Madinat Jumeirah (see 📍 Map p70, A3) capture Dubai's traditional wind-tower architecture, Creek activity and street life. They are available in colour and black-and-white and make great mementos. (Souq Madinat Jumeirah, Al-Sufouh Rd, Umm Suqeim 3; ⏱9am-11pm)

Lata's
ARTS & CRAFTS

Located at Souq Madinat Jumeirah (see 📍 Map p70, A3), this is our favourite one-stop shop for Arabian and Middle Eastern souvenirs, such as lamps, brass coffee pots, antique Bedouin *khanjars* (traditional curved daggers) and gorgeous Quran holders. It also has some fabulous silver jewellery and some not-so-fabulous fake costume stuff: let the knowledgeable staff know your taste straight up and they won't push the tacky stuff. (Souq Madinat Jumeirah, Al-Sufouh Rd, Umm Suqeim 3)

☑ Top Tip
Flea Market

If you've timed your visit right, then don't miss the monthly flea market, held from October to May on the first Saturday of the month at Al-Safa Park. Given the number of expats living in Dubai and given the fact that it is largely a transient society, you can get some real deals here. And, let's face it, there is something tantalising about seeking out treasures amid piles of pre-loved clothing, furniture, toys, home appliances, electronics, art, books and all that other stuff that's spilled out of local closets.

Understand
Carpet Buying 101

Due diligence is essential for prospective carpet buyers. Though you may only want a piece to match your curtains, you'll save a lot of time and money if you do a little homework.

Dealers will hype knot density, weave quality and country of origin, but really, these aspects are not the most important. The crucial thing to find out is how the wool was treated. A rug made with acid-treated wool will never look as good as it did the day you bought it. Conversely, a properly made rug will grow more lustrous in colour over time and will last centuries.

Here's a quick test. Stand atop the rug with rubber-soled shoes and do the twist. Grind the fibres underfoot. If they shed, it's lousy wool. You can also spill water onto the rug. See how fast it absorbs. Ideally it should puddle for an instant, indicating a high presence of lanolin. Best of all, red wine will not stain lanolin-rich wool.

National Iranian Carpets
CARPETS

This exceptional carpet business at Souq Madinat Jumeirah (see ◉ Map p70, A3) deals in the finest-quality Iranian carpets (the best in the world), and its patient and knowledgeable staff will give you all the time in the world to ensure you find the right carpet. It's in their best interests, after all. Bring photos of your home and they'll happily try to match your decor and style. (Souq Madinat Jumeirah, Al-Sufouh Rd, Umm Suqeim 3)

The Camel Company
SOUVENIRS

Your one-stop camel-souvenir shop at Souq Madinat Jumeirah (see ◉ Map p70, A3) stocks cute camels in every conceivable texture and form – fluffy camels in Hawaiian shirts, pink camels in tutus and plush ones so huggable you won't want to let them go – along with camel-themed notebooks, mouse pads, greeting cards, T-shirts, coffee mugs and more. (Souq Madinat Jumeirah, Al-Sufouh Rd, Umm Suqeim 3; ⊙10am-11pm)

O' de Rose
ART & CRAFTS

8 🔒 Map p70, C3

The antithesis of the cookie-cutter malls, this delightful boutique is set in a homey residential villa. Run by Lebanese-born fashion designer Mimi Shakhashir, you'll find all sorts of ethnic-chic creations here, ranging from hand-painted ceramics to hand-blown Syrian vases. Customers are greeted with a glass of refreshing O' de Rose (rose-flower drink); set aside plenty of time to browse. (www.o-derose .com; 999 Al-Wasl Rd, Umm Suqeim 2)

PETER ADAMS/CORBIS ©

Dubai carpet salesman

Garderobe
VINTAGE FASHION

9 Map p70, E2

This is the place to come to snag a one-off vintage item at an affordable price. The secondhand designerwear and accessories are in tip-top condition and typically include items by Chanel, Hermès, Alexander Wang and Gucci. The vintage concept has proved a big hit here, particularly among the expatriate community. (www.garderobevintage.com; Jumeirah Beach Rd, Umm Suqeim 1)

If
FASHION

10 Map p70, F2

Already a smash hit in Beirut and New York, this boutique is a fashion pioneer. It sells pieces by lesser-known designers, like Johnny Farah and Marc Le Bihan, that combine avant-garde haute couture with classic lines and fantastic accessories. (Umm Al-Sheif St, Umm Suqeim 1)

Explore

Sheikh Zayed Road

Sheikh Zayed Road lies at the very heart of Dubai's extraordinary meteoric development and is flanked by gleaming modern skyscrapers, including several of the city's iconic modern landmarks. The pinnacle is the Burj Khalifa, the tallest structure in the world: it's located at the epicentre of Downtown Dubai's most tantalising sights, namely the Dubai Mall, the Dubai Fountain and the Souq al-Bahar.

The Sights in a Day

☀ Plan to metro-and-taxi it to the Financial District, where there are plenty of cafes for those adrenalin-charged bankers. Spend an hour or so perusing the superb contemporary Middle Eastern art at the sophisticated galleries in **Gate Village** (p88) before hopping in a cab to the **Dubai Mall** (p82) to escape the hottest part of the day.

☀ Take the elevator to the top of the **Burj Khalifa** (p88) for incredible panoramic views, then tuck into a healthy salad at **Baker & Spice** (p90). Visit the watery wonderland of the **Aquarium** (p82) before perusing the shops. Wind up the afternoon by grabbing a restaurant pew at **Souq al-Bahar** (p88) overlooking the magical dancing fountains and set against a soaring Burj Khalifa backdrop.

☾ Enjoy more killer views (along with killer cocktails) at **Neos**, (p94), the high-octane bar at the hotel Address Downtown Dubai. Then head to the Emirates Towers for dinner at the legendary **Ivy** (p89) before showing off big time as you belt out your top Susan Boyle number at nearby **Harry Ghatto's** (p97).

For a local's day in Al-Quoz, see p84

◉ Top Sights
Dubai Mall (p82)

◯ Local Life
Al-Quoz (p84)

♥ Best of Dubai

Eating
Ivy (p89)

Baker & Spice (p90)

Drinking
Neos (p94)

Cin Cin's (p94)

Best Themed Attractions
Dubai Ice Rink (p96)

KidZania (p97)

Getting There

Ⓜ **Metro** The metro (Red Line) is useful for a number of sights on Sheikh Zayed Road. Main stops include Burj Khalifa/Dubai Mall, Emirates Towers and Dubai Marina.

Top Sights
Dubai Mall

The world's largest shopping centre, Dubai Mall is much more than the sum of its 1200 stores and 160 food outlets: it's a veritable family entertainment centre. The Mall is also unashamedly grandiose, with the world's largest indoor gold souq, a designer fashion avenue with dedicated catwalk and even its own glossy monthly magazine, *The Dubai Mall*. This is not a place you just nip in to for a tube of toothpaste: plan to spend several hours here.

👁 Map p86, B3

www.thedubaimall.com

Financial Centre Rd

🕙10am-10pm Sun-Wed, 10am-midnight Thu-Sat

Ⓜ Burj Khalifa/Dubai Mall (Red Line)

Dubai Aquarium

Don't Miss

Dubai Fountain

Against the backdrop of Burj Khalifa in the midst of a massive artificial lake, these choreographed dancing fountains are stunning. Water undulates as gracefully as a belly dancer, arcs like a dolphin and surges as high as 150m to a soothing soundtrack. There are plenty of great vantage points, including the bridge linking Souq al-Bahar with Dubai Mall, and the Dubai Mall terrace.

Dubai Aquarium

What could be a more fitting centrepiece for the world's largest shopping mall than a whopping three-storey aquarium with 33,000 marine creatures (including more than 400 sharks and rays), the world's largest aquarium window and a 48m walk-through tunnel with 270-degree views? If this isn't close enough for you, don a wetsuit and join a dive instructor on a shark dive or hop on a glass-bottomed boat for a glacial float.

Underwater Zoo

The very worthwhile Underwater Zoo contains three eco-zones – rainforest, rocky shore and living ocean – and a total of 38 aquatic displays. There are lots of rare and interesting denizens here, including air-breathing African lungfish, cheeky archerfish that catch insects by shooting water, spooky giant spider crabs and otherworldly sea dragons. Budget at least half an hour for both the aquarium tunnel and the zoo.

☑ Top Tips

▶ If you're driving to the Dubai Mall, don't forget that the car park is massive: be sure to collect a free ticket at the entrance which states the level on which you are parked.

▶ In the worst-case scenario, one of the attendants should be able to help find your car as there are cameras above every car.

▶ First thing: head for one of the information desks and pick up a free map.

▶ The Mall is busiest on Thursday and Friday evenings. If you don't like crowds, avoid these times.

✗ Take a Break

Enjoy a cup of frothy cappuccino and a classy pastry (or two) at the elegant **Emporio Armani Caffé** (p90)

If you're here with your (fussy) family, seek out the far-reaching culinary wizardry at **More** (p91)

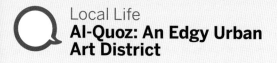

Local Life
Al-Quoz: An Edgy Urban Art District

Local artists and creative folk know that this is the exciting burgeoning zone for cutting-edge galleries and workshops, despite the on-the-surface anonymity of the industrial-style warehouses and dusty nondescript streets. Fortunately, a few decent restaurants are also appearing here, but it's still a challenging area, although undeniably compelling for anyone interested in art.

❶ Art Complex

One of the most established art centres here, the cultural complex of the **Courtyard** (www.courtyard-uae.com; 4B St; ⏱10am-6pm Sat-Thu) wraps around the eponymous courtyard flanked by an eccentric hodgepodge of buildings that resemble a miniature movie-studio backdrop: here an Arab fort, there a Moorish facade or an Egyptian tomb. The highlight is the bi-level gallery Total Arts at The Courtyard,

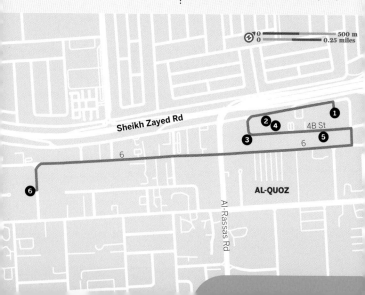

specialising in Middle Eastern art. Other spaces are occupied by a cafe, artist studios and various creative businesses.

➋ Cutting-Edge Art (and Champagne)

Talented young curators Sunny Rahbar and Claudia Cellini operate Dubai's most adventurous art space, **The Third Line** (www.thethirdline.com; Al-Quoz 3; ⏱11am-8pm Sat-Thu). The gallery consistently holds impressive exhibitions of contemporary Middle Eastern art, showcasing provocative work that often breaks the rules to create refreshing new forms. Sign up to the mailing list so you don't miss out on the glam champagne openings.

➌ More Provocative Art

Having carved a name for itself in the Dubai art scene, the **Gallery Isabelle van den Eynde** (www.ivde.net; 8 St; ⏱10am-2pm & 4-8pm Sat-Thu) showcases edgy and contemporary art from established and rising talent in the Middle Eastern region. Like so many in these parts, the gallery's exhibition spaces are set in a converted industrial warehouse with plenty of space.

➍ Lime Tree Cafe

This branch of the enormously successful minichain **Lime Tree Cafe** (4B St; snacks Dh15-25; ⏱7.30am-6pm) provides an invaluable opportunity for escaping the heat (there's no shade in Al-Quoz) and has evolved as a handy central meeting place for local

gallery-owners and artists. As always, it offers an irresistible choice of salads, quiches, focaccias and wraps, plus that legendary best-in-town carrot cake. The coffee and much of the produce is organic.

➎ For Cartoon Fans

Located a couple of doors away from the cafe, the entertaining **Cartoon Art Gallery** (www.cartoonartgallery.org; ⏱10am-6pm Sat-Thu) is the first gallery dedicated to cartoons in the Middle East. Typical temporary exhibitions are of artwork and posters illustrating the world of Tintin, as well as animated cartoons by such illustrious artists as the Japanese Hayao Miyazaki. You can grab a cup of coffee here, as well.

➏ Pick up a Paintbrush

If viewing all this art is bringing out your Picasso side, then make a detour to the **Jam Jar** (www.thejamjardubai.com; ⏱10am-8pm Mon-Thu & Sat, 2-8pm Fri), which, as well as being a superb gallery exhibiting contemporary art by emerging local and international talent, doubles as a DIY painting studio, popular with local potential artists. For a paltry few dirhams you can rent an easel, a canvas and all the paint and paper you require to create your own masterpiece.

JADDAF

*Dubai Creek
(Khor Dubai)*

Oud Metha Rd

3 Ras al-Khor
Wildlife
Sanctuary

AL-MARQADH

RAS AL-KHOR

13 Nad al-
Sheba Racecourse

0   1 km
0   0.5 miles

For reviews see

◆ Top Sights	p82
◉ Sights	p88
✕ Eating	p89
🍷 Drinking	p94
✸ Entertainment	p96
🛍 Shopping	p98

A   B   C   D   E

5   6   7   8

Sights

Souq al-Bahar   MALL

1 Map p86, B2

Designed in contemporary Arabian style, this attractive souq-style shopping centre, next to the iconic Dubai Mall, is Downtown Dubai's answer to Madinat Jumeirah. Meaning 'Market of the Sailor', it features natural stone walkways, high arches and seating overlooking the Dubai Fountain at several of its restaurants and bars, including Baker & Spice. (www.soukalbahar.ae; Exit 32, Sheikh Zayed Rd; ◷10am-10pm Sat-Thu, 2-10pm Fri)

Burj Khalifa   BUILDING

2 Map p86, B2

The Burj Khalifa is a groundbreaking feat of architecture and engineering. The world's tallest building pierces the sky at 828m and opened in January 2010, only six years after excavations began. Inside is a mix of offices and

---

Local Life
Art Nights
Don the smock-and-beret look and head for an Art Night at **Gate Village** (Map p86; C1; Sheikh Zayed Rd) in the Dubai International Financial Centre (DIFC), the hub of sophisticated contemporary art. This hip monthly event attracts a who's who in the local art world. Contact Art Dubai (www.artdubai.ae) for the next date.

---

apartments; the building is also home to the Armani Hotel – the first hotel to be designed and developed by Giorgio Armani. For visitors, the main attraction is the observation deck, 'At the Top', on the 124th floor. Admission is by reservation only. (www.burjkhalifa.ae; Dubai Mall, Financial Centre Rd; adult/over 12yr/under 12yr Dh100/75/free; ◷10am-10pm Sun-Wed, 10am-midnight Thu-Sat; ♿)

Ras Al-Khor Wildlife Sanctuary   NATURE RESERVE

3 Map p86, D5

Spy on Dubai's pink flamingo population of 3000-plus, which flocks here during the winter months, from excellent viewing hides. Powerful binoculars can be borrowed at the viewing hides to get a close-up of the birds without disturbing them. The juxtaposition of these elegant birds against the Dubai metropolis is amazing. Groups of five or more must apply to the Environment Department at the Municipality (located near the Deira main post office) for a permit at least two days before visiting. You can download an application form from www.wildlife.ae. (☎04-338 2324; off Oud Metha Rd; admission free; ◷9am-4pm Sat-Thu)

Cuadro   GALLERY

4 Map p86, C2

In a fabulous space taking up the entire ground floor of Gate Village's Bldg 10, this highly regarded gallery presents exciting contemporary artists

SYLVAIN SONNET/CORBIS ©

The Gate Building (designed by Gensler) and financial district

and sculptors from both the West and the Middle East. It also screens art-house films and organises workshops. (www.cuadroart.com; Gate Village, Bldg 10; ⊙10am-9pm Sun-Thu, noon-6pm Sat)

The Opera Gallery
GALLERY

For big spenders, this gallery near Cuadro (see 4 ⊙ Map p86, C2) at Gate Village has a small downstairs gallery with works by such masters as Picasso, Miró and Chagall. Other work typically includes large canvases by Middle Eastern contemporary artists, as well as sculpture, furniture and photography. The gallery also organises such major art events as the exhibition of Salvador Dalí sculptures that was held in Dubai Mall in November 2011. (www.operagallery.com; Gate Village, Bldg 3; ⊙10am-8pm Sun-Thu)

Eating

Ivy
BRITISH $$$

Dark oak panelling, soft green leather upholstery and stunning chandeliers set the retro-chic scene for a dining experience that includes classic British dishes like shepherd's pie and nostalgic sweet treats including baked Alaska and sticky toffee pudding. The Ivy, located at the Boulevard at Jumeirah Emirates Towers (see 14 🔒 Map p86, D1), is not as pricey as its celeb-clientele packaging may suggest (the business lunch

is a great deal). (📞04-319 8767; www
.theivy.ae; The Boulevard, Jumeirah Emirates
Towers, Sheikh Zayed Rd; mains Dh100-180)

Baker & Spice
INTERNATIONAL $$

Chunky wood furniture, a warm
ochre-and-pale-green colour scheme,
rows of white orchids and a novel
fruit-and-veg display over the bar set
the scene for one of the best healthy-
eating options in the city, located at
Souq al-Bahar (see 1 ◉ Map p86, B2). The
menu incorporates organic local pro-
duce whenever possible. Typical mains
include mushroom linguine with wild
prawns, and scallops with a beetroot-
and-orange salad and pomegranate
dressing. (Souq al-Bahar, Sheikh Zayed Rd;
mains Dh48-85)

La Petite Maison
FRENCH $$

It has been said that France's famed
Cuisine Niçoise is so hard to master
because it is so simple, relying
mainly on the freshness and seas-
onality of the ingredients. A relative
newcomer on Dubai's continental
dining scene, La Petite Maison, near
Cuadro (see 4 ◉ Map p86, C2), has got it
right, serving exquisite classic dishes
like onion tart and pasta with beef
ragout and mushrooms. (📞04-439
0505; Gate Village, Bldg 8, Sheikh Zayed Rd;
mains Dh75-95)

Rivington Grill
BRITISH $$$

If you're planning a dinner here, call
ahead to snag a table on the candlelit
terrace overlooking the fountains at
Souq al-Bahar (see 1 ◉ Map p86, B2). The

✅ Top Tip
Ice-Cream Cool-Down
Dubai Mall is home to some of
the best ice cream in town. Elbow
your way to any of the following for
some gelato time out:

Cold Stone Creamery Some
wonderful fruity flavours, plus one-
offs, like peanut-butter cup.

The Frozen Yoghurt Factory Go
healthy, sort of, with one of the
creamy choices here.

Milano The Italians have got it
right. Delicious gelato in lots of
flavours.

Morelli's Gelato Another surefire
Italian place with the same creamy
fab flavours.

grub is deliciously upmarket Brit,
with beef wellington, smoked had-
dock fish cakes, Lancashire hotpot,
and bubble and squeak, together with
poshed-up mushy peas. There is also
a classic (Sunday) roast served on
Saturday. Reservations recommended.
(📞04-423 0903; Souq al-Bahar, Sheikh
Zayed Rd; mains Dh85-140)

Emporio Armani Caffé
ITALIAN $$

The revolution in Dubai's mall food
offers no better example than this
outpost of the Armani empire at the
Dubai Mall (see ◉ Map p86, B3). The coffee
is as smooth as an Italian waiter, the
food is as stylishly presented as the
staff and the Italian flavours are so

good we wish they had a liquor licence. (Dubai Mall, Doha St; mains Dh55-150; ☺10am-11.30pm Sat-Thu, 2pm-midnight Fri)

Asado ARGENTINE $$$

 5 Map p86, A2

Meat-lovers will be in bovine heaven at this cheerful, lusty steakhouse. Choose your quality cut of tenderloin, veal chop, rib eye or sirloin from a tray brought to your table by servers clad in gaucho style. Then sit back and savour the delicious bread, the views of Burj Khalifa (sit on the terrace) and the sultry tunes from the live band. (✆04-428 7971; Palace-The Old Town, Emaar Blvd; mains Dh110-290; ☺dinner)

More INTERNATIONAL $$

This jazzy, industrial-style space in Dubai Mall (see ◉ Map p86, B3) draws a congenial mix of locals, expats and tourists. The menu hopscotches around the world – from Thai curries and Italian pastas to Spanish paella, veggie stir-fries and fat burgers. Breakfast is served all day. The restaurant has mushroomed to eight branches over the last couple of years. (Dubai Mall, Doha St; mains Dh30-70; ☺8am-10pm; ✈♟)

Noodle House ASIAN $$

For consistently good Asian food at reasonable prices, brave the crowds and the long communal wooden tables, tick your choice on a menu pad (you can't go wrong with a curry laksa), then kick back with an Asian beer or a glass of wine. There are now four other branches around town, including at the Boulevard at Jumeirah Emirates Towers (see 14 🔒 Map p86, D1), in Souq Madinat Jumeirah and Dubai Mall. (The Boulevard, Jumeirah Emirates Towers; mains Dh30-66; ☺noon-11.30pm; ✈♟)

Understand
Tax-Free Dubai: What it Means

When people talk about Dubai being tax-free, they are referring to personal income tax on wages. There are, however, import duties. There's been talk of creating a consumer tax, but at press time there was still none. Does this mean that a new Donna Karan suit will cost less here than in Milan, New York or London? Not necessarily, if you are shopping for mid- and low-cost goods and cars. But if you're in the market for, say, a new Rolex, you will save a bundle in Dubai. Otherwise, don't be lulled by the tax-free promise. Find what you want at home, then price it in Dubai. You may pay more in over-weight luggage charges that you wind up saving in the first place.

Gourmet Burger Kitchen

BURGERS $

6 Map p86, C1

This patty-and-bun UK import stacks its burgers so high you risk dislocating your jaw when trying to bite into one. Go classic or try one of the more adventurous choices, like the Kiwi Burger with beetroot, egg, pineapple and cheddar, inspired by the founders' New Zealand origins. (Level B1, Dubai International Financial Centre; burgers Dh28-34; ⊙9am-10pm Sat-Wed, to 11pm Thu & Fri; ⛄)

Zaatar W Zeit

LEBANESE $

7 Map p86, C1

In the wee hours, this Lebanese fast-food joint near Shangri-La Hotel is full of night owls hoping to restore balance to the brain with *manaeesh* (flat bread) topped with cheese, tomatoes, minced meats or, of course, *zaatar* (thyme, sesame, marjoram and oregano). Other branches are in Dubai Mall, Mall of the Emirates and on The Walk at JBR. (Sheikh Zayed Rd; mains Dh7-33; ⊙24hr; ⛄)

Rib Room

STEAKHOUSE $$$

Surrender to your inner carnivore at this power-player hangout at the Boulevard at Jumeirah Emirates Towers (see **14** Map p86, D1). The succulent cuts of aged steaks, juicy prime rib and chateaubriand speak for themselves, but even the more complicated dishes, such as braised Wagyu beef cheeks in port wine, arrive without needless

Breaking the fast at the end of Ramadan

Understand

Religion on a Plate

You may start to crave pork once you travel to Dubai and are rarely offered any. As an alternative to pork bacon, some supermarkets sell beef bacon and turkey bacon, but hypermarkets like Carrefour have dedicated 'pork rooms' that sell the real thing but are generally not entered by Muslims. To serve pork in a restaurant, you must have a pork licence. Likewise with alcohol, which is generally only served in hotels. If an item on a restaurant menu has been prepared with either alcohol or pork, it must be clearly marked.

Haram & Halal

Muslims never eat pork: it is haram, forbidden by Islam – purely for health reasons, as pigs are considered 'unclean'. Alcohol is forbidden, not for health, but because it makes followers forgetful of God and prayer. The other major dietary restriction applies to meat: it must be halal, meaning religiously suitable or permitted. The animal must be drained of its blood at the time of slaughter by having its throat cut. That is why much of the red meat slaughtered and sold locally is very pale in colour. In restaurants, you will easily find non-halal beef – just don't expect your tenderloin to be wrapped in a fatty strip of bacon before it's grilled.

Ramadan

And then there is Ramadan... when Muslims are required to fast and everyone, regardless of religion, is expected to observe the fast when in public. That means no eating, drinking or smoking during daylight hours. Some hotels still serve breakfast and lunch, but this is in specially designated rooms; most of the time eating during the day means room service or self-catering. Non-Muslims offered coffee or tea when meeting a Muslim during the fast should initially refuse politely, however, if your host insists, you should accept.

Ramadan would seem to be the ideal time to lose weight, yet a lot of locals pile on the pounds. For many, avoiding food from dawn to dusk results in immense hunger come sunset, and with hundreds of restaurants putting on good-value *iftar* (breaking the fast after sundown) buffets, the temptation to overindulge is everywhere.

flights of fancy. (☑04-319 8088; The Boulevard, Jumeirah Emirates Towers, Sheikh Zayed Rd; mains Dh115-160; ⊙lunch Sat-Thu, dinner daily)

Trader Vic's
ASIAN $$$

8 ✗ | Map p86, D1

This branch of the Polynesian-themed chain is one of the originals. Start at the bar with a cocktail – a lethal Mai Tai or a Potted Parrot (you can keep the ceramic bird) – before ordering from the Asian-inspired menu. The salmon is delicious, as are the Peking duck pancakes, while the cocktails and live band make dinner a party. (☑04-331 1111; Crowne Plaza Hotel; mains Dh85-130)

Organic Foods & Cafe
SUPERMARKET $

Despite the massive amounts of jet fuel required to ship them in, the fruits and veggies are 100% organic at Dubai's first natural supermarket at Dubai Mall (see ⊙ Map p86, B3). And that's not all: this shop is vast, with an extensive selection of organic packaged goodies, as well as freshly baked bread, a cheese section, butchers and even a 'pork room'. Environmentally friendly kiddie wear made by Bornsage is also available here. (ground fl, Dubai Mall, Doha St)

Candylicious
SWEETS $

Stand under the lollipop tree, guzzle a root-beer float at the soda fountain or soak up the tempting aroma of Garretts' gourmet popcorn at this colourful candy emporium at Dubai Mall (see ⊙ Map p86, B3). The 1000th store to open in Dubai Mall, it's stocked to the rafters with everything from humble jelly beans to gourmet chocolate from France and Switzerland. Pure bliss. Just don't tell your dentist. (ground fl, Dubai Mall)

Drinking

Neos
COCKTAIL BAR

9 ♟ | Map p86, B3

This glitzy sky-high bar on the 63rd floor, near Dubai Mall, has stunning floor-to-ceiling views of the world's tallest tower, the Burj Khalifa. But the art deco decor – fibre-optic light curtains, shiny black granite, crystal chandeliers, polished stainless-steel columns – and excess of beautiful people (do they come with the fittings?) might vie for your attention. Be impressed. (The Address, Downtown Dubai; ⊙6pm-2am)

Cin Cin's
BAR

10 ♟ | Map p86, E1

This chic spot with a stunningly lit bar and ice buckets that change colour (yes, that's right) has Dubai's finest wines-by-the-glass list and its best bar food. The freshly shucked oysters are tempting, or try the divine Wagyu beef burger flight: assorted tiny burgers served with rosemary and sea-salted fries. To round off the evening, retire to the cigar lounge

Understand
Role of Women

Gender roles are changing in Dubai, with more and more women wanting to establish careers before marriage. With successful Emirati women – such as the UAE minister of trade, Sheikha Lubna al-Qasimi (one of the most powerful women in the world according to *Forbes* magazine) and Dr Amina Rostamani (CEO of TECOM, a corporation that oversees several free-trade zones) – serving as role models, women's contribution to the workforce has grown considerably in the past decade.

An indirect byproduct of the shifting role of women is the ongoing trend for Emirati men to marry foreign women. One reason is that Emirati women are becoming better educated and, as a result, are less willing to settle down in the traditional role of an Emirati wife. Other contributing factors are the prohibitive cost of a traditional wedding, plus the dowry the groom must provide – essentially, it can save a lot of dirhams to marry a foreign girl.

with an excellent cognac. (The Fairmont Hotel, Sheikh Zayed Rd; ☺6pm-2am)

Agency
WINE BAR

At the Boulevard at Jumeirah Emirates Towers (see **14** 🔒 Map p86, D1), this stylish wine bar has an extensive wine list, excellent vintages by the glass, themed tasting selections and delicious tapas-size snacks – all of which keep it busy, particularly on weeknights, when it gets popular with the besuited Emirates Towers set. (The Boulevard, Jumeirah Emirates Towers, Sheikh Zayed Rd; ☺noon-3am Sun-Thu, 3pm-3am Sat)

iKandy
LOUNGE

11 🍸 Map p86, B1

White cushions on rattan lounges, filmy gauze curtains, soft lighting

and trance vibes set the mood at this rooftop, poolside chill-out bar. The billowing white curtains create intimate areas, and the stars, cocktails and *sheesha* make this a great wind-down (or wind-up) to the evening. (Shangri-La Hotel, Sheikh Zayed Rd; ☺6pm-2am Oct-May)

Vu's Bar
BAR

Located at the Jumeirah Emirates Towers (see **14** 🔒 Map p86, D1), Vu's Bar draws the tourists up the glass elevator with its stupendous views of Dubai. But residents come for the decent wines by the glass, stylish setting and buzzy atmosphere. (51st fl, Jumeirah Emirates Towers, Sheikh Zayed Rd; ☺noon-2.30am)

Blue Bar

LIVE MUSIC

12 Map p86, D1

Cool cats of all ages gather in this relaxed joint for some of the finest jazz and blues in town. It's tucked away in a ho-hum business hotel, but inside, all is forgiven. The mostly local talent starts performing at 10pm, so get there early to snag a table. (Novotel World Trade Centre, Sheikh Zayed Rd; ⏱2pm-2am)

Entertainment

Dubai Ice Rink

SKATING

There's something pleasurably ironic about ticking off a winter-sports checklist in a shopping mall in the Arabian desert. After tearing down the slopes at Ski Dubai, strap on a pair of skates at this Olympic-size indoor ice rink at Dubai Mall (see ◉ Map p86, B3). Rather not be the entertainment? Look out for upcoming ice-hockey matches and figure-skating events. (☎04-437 3111; www.dubaiicerink.com; Dubai Mall, Doha St; 1hr group lessons Dh35, 2hr public sessions Dh50, children under 5yr Dh15; ⏱10am-midnight)

Meydan Racecourse

RACECOURSE

13 ⭐ Map p86, A7

Opened in 2010, this spectacular racecourse is about 5km southwest of Sheikh Zayed Road. Spanning 1.6km, it has a solar- and titanium-panelled roof, can accommodate up to 60,000 spectators and integrates a five-star hotel, the Sky Bubble 360° vista restaurant and an IMAX theatre. There's a free-admission area where dress is casual. For the grandstand you'll need tickets and should dress to the nines. For online racing schedules and tickets, visit the Dubai Racing Club's website. (☎04-327 0077; www.dubairacingclub.com; Al-Meydan Rd)

Talise

SPA

Finally, a spa squarely aimed at stressed and jetlagged executives in need of revitalisation. Situated at the Boulevard at Jumeirah Emirates Towers (see 14 🏢 Map p86, D1), Talise has the usual range of massages and spa treatments, plus a few exotic ones. Kickstart your capillaries in the Oxygen Lounge (Dh85/165/330 per 15/30/60 minutes) or trick your body into believing it got eight hours of sleep by spending one in a flotation pool

---

✅ Top Tip

Beating the Drum

Here's an environmentally friendly, social and entertaining way of seeing the desert: join a drum circle. **Dubai Drums** (www.dubaidrums.com) hosts regular full-moon drum circles (adult/child Dh200/100) in desert camps. These sessions usually last several hours and occasionally until the early hours of the morning. Watch for the near-legendary all-nighter event. Drums and a barbecue dinner are provided.

DAVID BURTON/ALAMY ©

Dubai Ice Rink

(Dh330). (☏04-319 8181; www.jumeirah
.com/talise; The Boulevard, Jumeirah Emirates
Towers, Sheikh Zayed Rd; ⊙9am-11pm)

Harry Ghatto's   KARAOKE BAR

Knock back a couple of drinks if you
need to loosen your nerves before
belting out your best tune at this
beloved karaoke bar in the same
tower where Sheikh Mohammed has
his office: Jumeirah Emirates Towers (see **14** 🔒 Map p86, D1). Drinks are
expensive and service only so-so, but
we love the odd mix of people drawn
here, including the occasional local in
dishdasha (man's shirt-dress worn in
Kuwait and the UAE). (The Boulevard,
Jumeirah Emirates Towers, Sheikh Zayed Rd;
⊙8pm-3am)

KidZania   THEME PARK

A real winner with the kiddies, this
interactive miniature city at the
Dubai Mall (see 🗺 Map p86, B3) has
offices, a school, a racetrack, a fire
station, a hospital, a bank and other
real-world places. Children dress up
and playfully explore what it's like
to be a firefighter, doctor, mechanic,
pilot or other professional; there
are 70 roles to choose from. Older
kids can check out the nearby **Sega
Republic** theme park, which is sure
to be equally thrilling, with lots of
terrific – and speedy – rides. (www
.kidszania.com; 2nd fl, Dubai Mall, Doha St;
⊙10am-10pm Sun-Wed, to midnight Thu-Sat)

Shopping

Dubai Mall
SHOPPING MALL

Dubai's biggest and best mall (see ◉ Map p86, B3) has all the shops you could possibly want under one (or rather, several) roofs, including designer shops, international chains, Emirati speciality stores and souvenir shops. For more on this iconic mall, see p82. (www.thedubaimall.com; Doha St, off Sheikh Zayed Rd; ⏰10am-10pm Sun-Wed, to midnight Thu-Sat; 🛜)

The Boulevard at Jumeirah Emirates Towers
SHOPPING MALL

14 🔒 Map p86, D1

This exclusive shopping arcade in Emirates Towers is home to swish designer boutiques such as Armani and Gucci on the ground level and Pucci and Jimmy Choo upstairs, along with local favourite, the chic Boutique 1. Noodle House (p91) is here when you

---

Local Life
The Friday Mall Experience
Where are all the locals? You may occasionally wonder where all the local Emiratis are, particularly if you are staying in Bur Dubai, Deira or at a tourist complex or beach hotel. But one place where you can be sure to see hundreds of local families is at Dubai Mall on a Friday evening. The later the better – it is open to midnight.

---

need to refuel, as is The Agency (p95), for shopping postmortems. (The Boulevard, Jumeirah Emirates Towers, Sheikh Zayed Rd; ⏰10am-10pm Sat-Thu, 4-10pm Fri; 🛜)

Kinokuniya
BOOKS

If you forgot to pack your iPad or your Kindle, never fear, this massive 68,000-sq-ft bookstore on the 2nd floor of Dubai Mall (see ◉ Map p86, B3) stocks over half a million books and a thousand magazines in English, Arabic, Japanese, French, German and Chinese. It is also home to a pleasant cafe with superb fountain views. (2nd fl, Dubai Mall, Doha St)

Azza Fahmy Jewellery
JEWELLERY

Egyptian Azza Fahmy's coveted jewellery, here at the Boulevard at Jumeirah Emirates Towers (see **14** 🔒 Map p86, D1), draws on Islamic and Arab traditions, combining classical Arabic poetry and Islamic wisdom in fine calligraphy with gemstones, beads and motifs, using elements from different ages and civilisations. Souvenirs don't come more precious than this. (The Boulevard, Jumeirah Emirates Towers, Sheikh Zayed Rd)

Boutique 1
FASHION

The sexy *2001: A Space Odyssey* interior is reason enough to visit this chic one-stop designer shop at the Boulevard at Jumeirah Emirates Towers (see **14** 🔒 Map p86, D1). It's an added bonus that its curvy capsule-like boutiques are home to the hottest fashion, including pieces by Alexander

Understand
Global Village

This carnival-like event runs from late November to late February about 13km south of Sheikh Zayed Road. Think of it as a sort of World Fair for shoppers. Each of the 30-something pavilions showcases a specific nation's culture and – of course – products. Some favourites: the Afghanistan pavilion, for fretwork-bordered stone pendants and beaded-silver earrings; Palestine, for traditional cross-stitch *kandouras* (casual shirt-dresses worn by men and women) and ever-popular cushion covers; Yemen, for its authentic *khanjars* (traditional curved daggers); and Kenya for its kitschy bottle-top handbags. Dig the earnest entertainment, from Chinese opera to Turkish whirling dervishes. Check the website (www.globalvillage.ae) for more info.

McQueen, Easton Pearson, Elie Saab and Missoni. (The Boulevard, Jumeirah Emirates Towers, Sheikh Zayed Rd)

Emilio Pucci   FASHION
Dubai's first Pucci store, at the Boulevard at Jumeirah Emirates Towers (see 14 🔒 Map p86, D1), is worth visiting just for the groovy interior, but you'll also find a colourful and funky range of psychedelic fashion, accessories and handbags – more affordable here than anywhere. (The Boulevard, Jumeirah Emirates Towers, Sheikh Zayed Rd)

Hamleys   TOYS
London's famous toy store, Hamleys, is kiddie heaven, and heaven has come to Dubai. Located at Dubai Mall (see 🔘 Map p86, B3), it has everything that squeaks, bleeps, whizzes and chimes – including the staff – in this mega toy paradise. Only Scrooge would fail to be enthralled. Bring a little person to blend in. (Dubai Mall, Doha St)

Jimmy Choo   SHOES
The shoes that found fame on the feet of sexy sitcom stars are now a household name in Dubai. Seek out the source at the Boulevard at Jumeirah Emirates Towers (see 14 🔒 Map p86, D1). Recline on the chaise longue at the fabulous flagship store so you can see the miracles these heavenly creatures work. (The Boulevard, Jumeirah Emirates Towers, Sheikh Zayed Rd)

Taharan Persian Carpets & Antiques   GIFTS
This shop, located on the 1st floor of Souq al-Bahar (see 1 🔘 Map p86, B2), has a misleading name: in addition to the carpets and a handful of antiques, there are superb Iranian decorative items, including delicately carved boxes made from gorgeous peacock-turquoise and blue decorative plates, fancy stained-glass lamps and plenty of colourful silver jewellery and trinkets. (www.pch.ae; Souq al-Bahar)

Explore

New Dubai

New Dubai is well named and most dramatically reflects the city's ability to reinvent itself, creating artificial islands out at sea and constructing a lofty thicket of skyscrapers from the desert. Home to the Palm Jumeirah, (another) huge shopping mall, flashy residential developments, a luxury marina and the city's best beach resorts, this is one of Dubai's most iconic and representative neighbourhoods.

The Sights in a Day

Early morning, hop on the metro to the Dubai Marina for breakfast at one of the many cafes overlooking the **Walk at JBR** (p106), followed by a leisurely stroll perusing the shops and people-watching. After a dip in the sea at Jumeirah Beach Residence's Open Beach, go *italiano* with lunch at the Hilton's **BiCE** (p110).

It's that hottest time of the day again, so cool down by taking to the ski slopes at **Ski Dubai** (p107), the extraordinary winter wonderland at the **Mall of the Emirates** (p116). Enjoy some après-ski retail therapy at the mall, then hop on the monorail to the Palm Jumeirah's Atlantis Hotel, home to the extraordinary **Lost Chambers** (p106), **Dolphin Bay** (p106) and the **Aquaventure** waterpark (p106).

Enjoy superb Moroccan food along with a suitably fezzed-up atmosphere at **Tagine** (p109) before heading for post-dinner drinks at the fabled **Buddha Bar** (p113) in the Grosvenor House hotel. Round off the night by gliding up the elevator to the hotel's 44th floor to the swanky retro-chic **Bar 44** (p112), which has a sweeping panorama, plus live blues and jazz.

For a local's Friday in New Dubai, see p102.

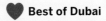

Local Life

Friday Brunch (p102)

Best of Dubai

Eating
Rhodes Mezzanine (p109)

Eauzone (p110)

Drinking
Bar 44 (p112)

Barasti Bar (p113)

Buddha Bar (p113)

Family Entertainment
Dolphin Bay (p106)

Aquaventure (p106)

Lost Chambers (p106)

Getting There

Ⓜ **Metro** The most useful metro stop is Dubai Marina (Red Line).

Local Life
Let's Do Brunch...

The Dubai work week runs from Sunday through Thursday. Friday is a day off for (nearly) everyone here, and Friday brunch is an expat institution. Virtually all hotel restaurants set up an all-you-can-eat buffet with an option for unlimited champagne or wine. Some smaller, independent restaurants also serve brunch, but without alcohol, making them popular with local families. Here's our shortlist for top brunches in town.

❶ For Seafood Lovers

The view of fancy yachts and a forest of sleek high-rises impresses almost as much as the all-time popular brunch at **Aquara** (☎ 04-362 7900; Dubai Marina Yacht Club, Marina Walk, Dubai Marina; brunches with soft/house/premium drinks Dh220/290/350; ⏰ 12.30-3.30pm Fri), which attracts local expats in their shoals. A fishy bonanza of sushi, sashimi, crabs, oysters, clams and cooked-to-order lobster are all

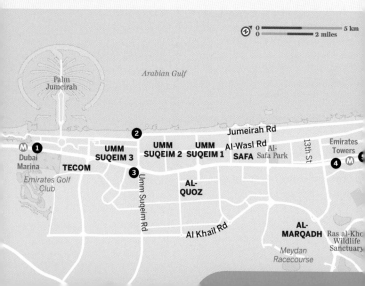

artistically presented. Don't forget to hit the dessert room. This brunch is extremely good value.

❷ Sublime Setting

Come to **Al-Qasr** (☎04-366 6730; Madinat Jumeirah; brunch with drinks Dh525; ⏱12.30-4pm) hungry to fully enjoy this unbelievable cornucopia of succulent and delicious meats, sushi, seafood, foie gras, beautiful salads, mezzes, all sorts of hot dishes, and more... It's one of the most expensive brunch feasts in town, but the quality and range justify the price tag. The setting is also hard to beat: you're surrounded by the Venetian-style canals of Madinat Jumeirah.

❸ Something for Everyone

A great choice for fussy families or a diverse group of friends, the giant food court at **Sezzam** (☎04-341 3600; Mall of the Emirates, Sheikh Zayed Rd; brunch without alcohol Dh150; ⏱12.30-3pm Fri; 👶) has several stations that dish up everything from freshly made sushi to burgers, pasta and pizza (including a saucy little choice topped with chicken tikka). This is a great venue for Friday brunch with the kids: entertainers and a bouncy castle keep them occupied. It's also notable for its setting – overlooking the adjacent Ski Dubai winter wonderland.

❹ An Asian Experience

One of an ever-increasing crop of contemporary Japanese restaurants, the dramatic bilevel **Zuma** (☎04-425 5660; Bldg 6, Gate Village, Financial District; brunches without/with alcohol Dh315/425; ⏱12.30-3pm Fri) is immensely popular for its pricey but top-notch brunch. Gorge on plump sushi, sashimi and oysters, nibble on juicy kebabs straight off the robata grill and try such signature dishes as crispy fried squid and blackened cod.

❺ East to West

Eight open kitchens serving up cuisine from around the globe may sound more food court than five-star, but **Spectrum on One** (☎04-332 5555; Fairmont Hotel; brunch with soft/house/premium drinks Dh295/395/550; ⏱noon-3pm; 👶) dishes up one of Dubai's most consistently good brunches. While it's still an odd sight to see one diner gobbling down fresh oysters while a companion tackles a green curry, the ability to sate disparate tastes with aplomb is this restaurant's forte. Other pluses are the free-flowing champagne and an entire room full of port and cheeses.

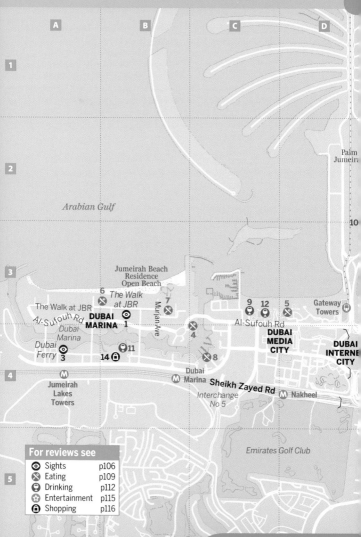

A
B
C
D

1

2

Palm
Jumeira

10

Arabian Gulf

3

Jumeirah Beach
Residence
Open Beach

6 **The Walk
at JBR**

The Walk at JBR

Al-Sufouh Rd

**DUBAI
MARINA** 1

*Dubai
Marina*

*Dubai
Ferry* 3

14 11

7

Murjan Ave

4

8

9 12 5

Al-Sufouh Rd

**DUBAI
MEDIA
CITY**

Gateway
Towers

**DUBAI
INTERNE
CITY**

Dubai
Marina

Sheikh Zayed Rd Nakheel

*Interchange
No 5*

4

Jumeirah
Lakes
Towers

Emirates Golf Club

5

For reviews see
◉ Sights   p106
✖ Eating   p109
🍷 Drinking   p112
★ Entertainment p115
🔒 Shopping   p116

E F G H

2

1

Arabian Gulf

2

3

Al-Sufouh Rd

4

AL-
SUFOUH

TECOM/Dubai
Internet
City Ⓜ

TECOM

AL-
BARSHA

Sheikh Zayed Rd

Ⓜ Sadaf

Interchange
No 4

Mall of the
Emirates Ⓜ

13 🔒

5

0   1 km
0   0.5 miles

Sights

Walk at JBR
OUTDOORS

1 Map p104, B3

Located in front of the Jumeirah Beach Residence, the city's first outdoor shopping and dining promenade encompasses more than 300 largely family-friendly restaurants, cafes, shops, supermarkets and boutiques. Tourists join local residents in strolling down the 1.7km stretch, watching the world on parade from a pavement cafe or browsing for knick-knacks at the Covent Garden Market (p116). (Dubai Marina; ⏱10am-10pm Sat-Thu, 3.30-10pm Fri; 🚶)

Dolphin Bay
DOLPHIN PARK

Dolphin Bay is the place to make friends with those sociable finny mammals known for their playfulness and intelligence. Touch, hug or kiss them in a shallow pool or catch a piggyback ride to the deeper waters of the lagoon. Combine a visit with a trip to nearby Aquaventure (see 2 Map p104, E1). Reserve via the website. (www.atlantisthepalm.com; Atlantis, The Palm, Palm Jumeirah; shallow-/deep-water interaction Dh790/975, incl same-day access to Aquaventure & private beach)

Aquaventure
AMUSEMENT PARK

2 Map p104, E1

Crowning the massive Palm, the flashiest hotel in Dubai boasts one of the largest water-themed parks in the world. Plunge down the Ziggurat – a 60ft drop into a shark-infested lagoon (protected by a transparent tunnel). (www.atlantisthepalm.com; Atlantis, The Palm, Palm Jumeirah; adult/child Dh285/220; ⏱10am-5pm)

Lost Chambers
AQUARIUM

This fantastic labyrinth of underwater halls, passageways and fish tanks near Aquaventure (see 2 Map p104, E1) re-creates the legend of the lost city of Atlantis. Some 65,000 exotic marine creatures inhabit 20 aquariums, where rays flutter and jellyfish

---

🔍 Local Life

The Royal Treatment

The Oriental Hammam at the **One&Only Spa** (Map p104, D3; ☎04-399 9999; www.oneandonly resorts.com; One&Only Royal Mirage Hotel, Al-Sufouh Rd, Al-Sufouh; treatment Dh360; ⏱8.30am-10pm) is a fabulous and authentic Moroccan bathhouse experience. Moroccan attendants walk you into a giant, steamy marble room lit by stained-glass lanterns, where they wrap you in muslin, bathe you on a marble bench and give you a thorough scrub. They then lead you to a steam room, where you relax before receiving an invigorating mud body mask, a honey facial, a brief massage and your final rinse. Afterwards, you're wrapped in dry muslin and escorted to a meditative relaxation room, where you drift off to sleep and awaken to hot mint tea and dates. Pure bliss!

Walk at JBR

dance, moray eels lurk, and pretty but poisonous lionfish float. The centre-piece is the 11-million-L Ambassador Lagoon. You can feed the rays (Dh175) or go on a guided tour (Dh75), but if you choose to do neither of the above, at least wander to the entrance where you can see one of the largest aquariums for free. (www.atlantisthepalm.com; Atlantis, The Palm, Palm Jumeirah; adult/under 12yr Dh100/70, combo ticket incl Aquaventure Dh250/200; ⏰10am-10pm; 👪)

Dubai Ferry
BOAT TOUR

3 ◎ Map p104, A4

One-hour boat trips depart from Marina Mall and take in several major sights, including Jumeirah Beach Park and Heritage Village.

Tickets can be bought on board. Don't worry if you get here early, as you can enjoy the views of the water flanked by a show-stopping selection of shimmering towers. (Water Transport Station, Marina Mall, Dubai Marina; tickets Dh75; ⏰11am, 5pm, 7pm & 9pm)

Ski Dubai
SKIING

Dubai's ski resort, at the Mall of the Emirates (see 13 🅱 Map p104, H5), has all bases covered: a children's snowpark, a gentle beginners' slope and the world's first indoor black run for those who like it steep. A quad lift takes skiers and boarders up to two stations, and there's a magic carpet for beginners. The snow uses no chemicals: it's 'real' snow that falls overnight at around -10°C. Just bring

Understand

Pitfalls in Paradise

Even in a city known for its outlandish megaprojects, the Palm Jumeirah stands out: an artificial island in the shape of a palm tree made from 1 billion cu metres of dredged sand and stone. Built to increase Dubai's beachfront, it consists of a 2km-long trunk and 16-frond crown, which are kept in place by an 11km-long crescent-shape breakwater. An elevated driverless monorail whisks passengers from the Gateway Towers station at the bottom of the trunk to Atlantis.

Plans & Delays

'May' is the operative word when it comes to the Palm Jumeirah. When construction began in 2001, developers envisioned a mix of five-star hotels, luxurious beachfront villas, high-rise apartment buildings, marinas and malls. But it soon became clear that not all was going according to plan. The completion date kept getting pushed back. After innumerable delays, at least one more hotel has opened – One&Only The Palm. The QE2, meanwhile, which was to be a floating hotel, will now relocate to Cape Town. Apparently, the amount of asbestos used in the original building of the luxury liner was potentially hazardous and a major factor in this decision.

Environmental Impact

The environmental impact of the Palm Jumeirah has been significant. Dredging had an adverse effect on local marine life, and the breakwater inhibited tidal movement, leading to stagnant water, excessive algae growth and smelly beaches. On a more positive note, the problem has since been somewhat alleviated by cutting gaps into the breakwater. Furthermore, well-publicised *New York Times* reports in 2009 stating that the Palm was sinking by 5mm per year have been categorically refuted by developers, Nakheel, who say that there have been no reports of any structural problems on any of the buildings.

Nakheel, which has been forced to shelve plans for additional islands due to massive debt, is keeping environmentalists happier with its latest project – building a string of artificial reefs off the city state's coast to attract more aquatic life.

a hat – all equipment is incorporated in the price, including disposable socks. Lessons cost from Dh140 per hour. (☑04-409 4000; www.skidxb.com; Mall of the Emirates, Sheikh Zayed Rd; admission plus ski slope adult/child Dh180/150; ☺10am-11pm Sun-Wed, 10am-midnight Thu, 9am-midnight Fri)

Softtouch Spa   SPA

After skiing the slopes next door, pamper your body in this luxury spa at the Mall of the Emirates (see **13** 🔒 Map p104, H5). It has tranquil Asian-minimalist interiors (slate floors, Thai silk walls and orange hanging lamps), Ayurvedic treatments, expert staff and beautiful Ligne St Barth products. (☑04-341 0000; www.kempinski-dubai.com; Kempinski Mall of the Emirates Hotel, Sheikh Zayed Rd; ☺9am-8pm)

Favourite Things   ACTIVITY CENTRE

These guys have it all covered: several areas and activities for children, a jungle gym, art and cooking classes, a sand room and a soft play area for tots, plus puppet shows and story time at weekends. Parents are not forgotten, with a cafe and shop selling all kinds of trendy and practical kiddie-geared wear and products. Located at Marina Mall (see **14** 🔒 Map p104, B4), it also has a dance studio with classes, ranging from classical ballet to hip hop, for children and adults. (www.favouritethings.com; Marina Mall, Dubai Marina; ☺9am-9pm)

Eating

Rhodes Mezzanine   BRITISH $$$

4 🍴 Map p104, C4

Celebrity chef Gary Rhodes is famous for bringing British cuisine into the 21st century and has a Michelin star to prove it. Here, the emphasis is squarely on quality ingredients prepared in fresh, surprising ways. There's fish on the menu, but it's meat-lovers who will discover culinary bliss in such dishes as the fillet steak, rack of lamb or slow-roasted pork belly. (☑04-317 6000; www.grosvenorhouse-dubai.com; Grosvenor House, Al-Sufouh Rd, Dubai Marina; ☺dinner Mon-Sat)

Tagine

MOROCCAN $$$

5 🍴 Map p104, D3

With the best Moroccan vibe in Dubai, Tagine transports you directly to Fez with its beautiful alcoves, arches and low, cushioned seating. Once inside the dimly lit cavern, waiters in fezzes (if they aren't dancing) serve up excellent versions of classics such as *harira* (soup based on meat, vegetables and pulses) and pigeon *pastilla* (pie). (☑04-399 9999; http://royalmirage.oneandonlyresorts.com; One&Only Royal Mirage, Al-Sufouh Rd, Al-Mina al-Seyahi; mains Dh75-170; ☺dinner Tue-Sun)

GIOVANNI SIMEONE/4CORNERS ©

Buddha Bar (p113)

Eauzone

INTERNATIONAL $$$

A romantic evening with adventurous cuisine awaits those making their way across the low-lit boardwalk to this alluring restaurant, set amid tranquil pools near Tagine (see 5 Map p104, D3). The contemporary menu takes some Asian-inspired diversions, but never enough to break the spell of the magic surrounds. It's best visited for dinner. (☎04-399 9999; http://royalmirage.oneandonlyresorts.com; One&Only Royal Mirage, Al-Sufouh Rd, Al-Mina al-Seyahi; mains Dh115-225)

BiCE

ITALIAN $$$

6 Map p104, B3

The godfather of Italian cuisine in Dubai is this understated, elegant restaurant at the Walk at JBR. The accomplished chef uses quality imported ingredients and treats them with respect – all too rare a combination in this city. Excellent breads, a well-selected wine list and a well-drilled staff help cement BiCE's reputation. (☎04-399 1111; www1.hilton.com; Hilton Dubai Jumeirah, Al-Sufouh Rd, Al-Mina al-Seyahi; mains Dh150-220; ☎)

Tiffinbites

INDIAN $$

Despite the name, a tiffin is considerably more satisfying than a mere bite: it is an entire meal that here comprises three separate bowls containing a curry, a vegetable dish and rice. This place, handily situated on the Walk at JBR (see 1 ⊙ Map p104, B3), pushes the 'we serve real Indian food' tagline and it seems spot on. Prices are fair and the quantities generous. The decor? Best described as a cross between a Bollywood set and an ice-cream parlour, but it somehow works. (www.tiffinbites.ae; The Walk at JBR, Dubai Marina; mains Dh30-60, tiffins Dh49)

Tribes

AFRICAN $$

At the Mall of the Emirates (see 13 🔒 Map p104, H5), here, at last, is a restaurant in a mall with muted lighting – all the better for appreciating the decor, with its shields, spears and faux-fur throws. The food is meat based, with steaks, plus some alternatives, including Mozambique prawns and Ugandan fish croquettes. Tribal Drumming is a regular floor show, which contributes to the out-of-Africa experience. (Mall of the Emirates, Sheikh Zayed Rd; mains Dh40-60; 👶)

Frankie's Italian Bar & Grill

ITALIAN $$

Look for the neon-lit movie-style sign with superchef Marco Pierre White as the star billing. Considering the celeb connections, this Italian restaurant, located on the Walk at JBR (see 1 ⊙ Map p104, B3), is comfortingly down to earth, with cosy russet tones, parquet flooring and nightly pianist. There is nothing nouveau about the huge pasta portions, either, and the traditional oven churns out decent pizzas as well. (📞04-396 7222; Oasis Beach Tower, The Walk at JBR, Dubai Marina; mains Dh80-130)

Maya

MEXICAN $$$

7 🍴 Map p104, B3

As soon as you taste the *real* margaritas here, you know you're in safe hands. This whimsically designed restaurant gives Mexican cuisine the respect it deserves. Try the guacamole prepared fresh at your table, the amazing chile relleno with seafood or the humble tortilla soup – so authentic it would make a Mexican grandmother weep. (📞04-399 5555; www.leroyalmeridien-dubai.com; Le Royal Méridien Beach Resort & Spa; mains Dh110-235; 🕐12.30-4pm Fri, 7.30pm-midnight Mon-Sat)

Q Local Life

Celebrity Chefs Come (& Go)

In August 2010 Gary Rhodes opened his second restaurant, a dedicated steakhouse: *Rhodes Twenty 10* at Le Royal Méridien Beach Resort & Spa, Dubai Marina. Meanwhile celeb chef wonder boy Jamie Oliver opened his first Dubai restaurant, Jamie's Italian, in Festival City in early 2012, at around the same time that Gordon Ramsay closed his Michelin-star Deira-based Verre and called it quits (at least at the time of writing) in Dubai.

Nina

INDIAN $$

Follow the locals to this lush den near Tagine (see 5 ✗ Map p104, D3), where the floor-to-ceiling purple fabric, red-orange light and beaded curtains create a seductive backdrop for the dynamic cooking on offer. The chef combines Indian with a touch of Thai and tempers it with European techniques. The results will perk up even the most passive proboscis: rich spicing means flavours develop slowly on the palate with an elegant complexity that demands savouring. (☎04-399 9999; http://royalmirage.oneandonlyresorts .com; One&Only Royal Mirage, Al-Sufouh Rd, Al-Mina al-Seyahi; mains Dh60-145; ☺dinner)

Almaz by Momo

MOROCCAN $$

Restaurateur Mourad 'Momo' Mazouz, creator of Sketch and Momo in London, has made what many consider an odd move by opening up in a mall in Dubai. But the diverse space here at the Mall of the Emirates (see 13 🔒 Map p104, H5) is a stunning success, offering a groovy *sheesha* room, a stylish salon for snacks and (nonalcoholic) drinks, a sophisticated restaurant serving up Maghrib classics, a Moroccan patisserie and a funky boutique. (☎04-409 8877; Mall of the Emirates, Sheikh Zayed Rd; mains Dh90-145)

Café Bateel

CAFE $$

8 ✗ Map p104, C4

When the gourmet date brand, Bateel, somehow lit on the idea of fusing Umbrian cuisine and Arabic coffee with the humble date, the result was a cafe

☑ Top Tip
What to Wear
You can't wear whatever you want. All that locals ask is that visitors dress respectfully, with clothes that are not too revealing. Locals will judge you on how you dress: guys in shorts at shopping malls will be assumed to have forgotten their pants and gals who reveal too much skin will cause offence. If you're going clubbing, take a taxi.

featuring dates in most dishes – with interesting results. Good coffee and delicious pastries go well with people-watching on the Marina Walk. (Marina Walk, Dubai Marina; ☺dinner)

Drinking

Bar 44

COCKTAIL BAR

While this sophisticated champagne and cocktail bar can appear dauntingly exclusive at first glance, the bar staff are friendly and regulars are made to feel like family. An elevator ride skywards from Rhodes Mezzanine (see 4 ✗ Map p104, C4), the bar has spectacular views. Drinks are pricey, but the sublime cocktails and fantastic views of New Dubai's skyscrapers and the marina more than compensate. (Grosvenor House, Al-Sufouh Rd, Dubai Marina; ☺6pm-2am)

Barasti Bar
BAR

9 🍸 Map p104, C3

With comfy rattan white-cushioned sofas on the wooden deck, this enormous alfresco beachside bar retains the laid-back atmosphere that first made it so popular with Dubai's residents. It's the perfect place to enjoy a drink watching the sun go down on a balmy evening. (www .lemeridien-minaseyahi.com; Le Méridien Mina Seyahi Beach Resort & Marina, Al-Sufouh Rd, Jumeirah; ⏱11.30am-1am)

Buddha Bar
BAR

If there are celebs in town, they'll show up at Buddha Bar, where the dramatic Asian-inspired interiors are decked out with gorgeous chandeliers, a wall of reflective sheer glass, and an enormous Buddha lording over the

Understand
Myth Busting

You can buy alcohol. As a visitor, you can buy drinks in bars and clubs (generally attached to four- and five-star hotels). But you can't buy alcohol to take back to your hotel – so stock up on duty-free on the way into Dubai. Non-Muslim expats need an alcohol licence, entitling them to a fixed monthly amount of alcohol (the more you earn, the higher your limit), which is available from low-key liquor outlets.

heathens. Drop in here after dining at nearby Rhodes Mezzanine (see 4 🍴 🔜 Map p104, C4). The bartenders put on quite a show with their impressive shakes. (Grosvenor House, Al-Sufouh Rd, Dubai Marina)

Après
LOUNGE

This funky low-key bar is Dubai's first in a mall, making it perfect for movie or shopping-spree postmortems. Adjacent to Ski Dubai at the Mall of the Emirates (see 13 🔒 Map p104, H5), with fabulous snowy vistas, it's also an ideal après-ski/snowboarding bar (obviously the idea). It does excellent cocktails with unusual ingredients – tobacco-infused rum, anyone? (Mall of the Emirates, Sheikh Zayed Rd; ⏱noon-1am)

Bidi Bondi
BAR

10 🍸 Map p104, D3

This unpretentious Aussie-themed sports bar is a rare find on the Palm's glitzy social scene. The outside area overlooks the beach and pool, while inside is a great venue for watching TV sports. Serves up no-nonsense *sangers* (sandwiches) and burgers, and is one of the few places to stock Bundaberg rum (aka Aussie rocket fuel). It's located between Buildings 3 and 4. (Shoreline Apartments 1-5, Palm Jumeirah; ⏱10am-midnight)

Maya
BAR

Arrive an hour before sunset to snag one of the Gulf-view tables on the rooftop bar of this upmarket Mexican

☑️ Top Tip

VIP Areas

Many nightclubs have VIP areas with extras like private waiters, free valet parking, tailor-made menus, a private bar, fully controllable sound and light system, specially tailored packages, complimentary limo and, generally, the best views in the venue, along with total privacy. Expect to pay around Dh3000 for these memorable special-occasion privileges.

restaurant, Maya (see 7 ⊗ Map 104, C4), at the Royal Méridien. Swill margaritas spiked with top-shelf tequila as the sun slowly slips into the sea. A plate of succulent duck enchiladas sure beats the nachos as the perfect booze antidote. (Le Royal Méridien Beach Resort & Spa; ⏲6pm-2am Mon-Sat)

Blends   BAR

11 🍸 Map p104, B4

The name is very fitting because Blends indeed folds three distinct libation stations into its 4th-floor space. Channel Ernest Hemingway in the clubby cigar room, complete with requisite leather sofa, dark woods and a coffered ceiling. For date night, the sultry, candlelit champagne bar, with its floor-to-ceiling windows, provides a suitable setting for quiet conversation. And finally, there's the trendy cocktail lounge. (The Address, Dubai Marina; ⏲4pm-1.30am)

Rooftop Bar   COCKTAIL BAR

With its Persian carpets, cushioned banquettes and Moroccan lanterns, the Rooftop Bar is a fantasy from *The Thousand and One Nights*. Add to that a soundtrack of oriental chill-out music and some of Dubai's best cocktails, and you have one of the city's most atmospheric bars. Book the romantic corner seat for special occasions and consider kick-starting the evening with a meal at downstairs Tagine (see 5 ⊗ Map p104, D3) first. (http://royalmirage.oneandonly resorts.com; One&Only Royal Mirage, Al-Sufouh Rd, Al-Mina al-Seyahi; ⏲5pm-1am)

Senyar   BAR

12 🍸 Map p104, C3

A secluded terrace, illuminated white walls, cherry-red furnishings and a glass staircase leading to a chic upstairs lounge make for a stylish bar. It can be a tad quiet, but with live music and a menu of speciality beers, exotic cocktails and tapas, this bar will kickstart a night out. (Westin Mina Seyahi, Al-Sufouh Rd; ⏲noon-1.30am Sat-Wed, to 2.30am Thu & Fri)

N'Dulge   CLUB

This sexy nightclub at the iconic Atlantis resort consists of three areas: one is the N'Dulge Arena, with its circular suspended catwalk used by circus performers, magicians, mimes, dancers, stilt walkers and the like. Another space is the alfresco terrace, while the restaurant serves sushi with a community-table option. There are also theme nights, fashion shows and guest DJs.

Find it near Aquaventure (see **2** 👁 Map p104, E1).(www.atlantisthepalm.com; Atlantis, The Palm, Palm Jumeirah; 🕑9.30pm-3am)

Entertainment

Dubai Community Theatre & Arts Centre (DUCTAC)

THEATRE

Filling a much-needed void in Dubai's cultural scene, DUCTAC hosts classical music, opera, drama, musicals and art exhibitions, along with art workshops. Much support is given to Emirati talent, making this a good place to plug into the local scene. Find it at the Mall of the Emirates (see **13** 🔒 Map p104, H5). (📞04-341 4777; www.ductac.org; level 2, Mall of the Emirates, Sheikh Zayed Rd; 🕑9am-10pm Sat-Thu, 11am-10pm Fri)

Sheesha Courtyard

SHEESHA BAR

It might take a connoisseur to appreciate all the different *sheesha* flavours on offer. But who wouldn't enjoy the aroma of apple *sheesha* reclining on cushions in this Arabian courtyard, particularly after dining at the adjacent Moroccan restaurant, Tagine (see **5** ✕ Map p104, D3), among palm trees flickering with fairy lights? (http://royalmirage.oneandonlyresorts.com; One&Only Royal Mirage, Al-Sufouh Rd, Al-Mina al-Seyahi; 🕑7pm-1am)

TRAVELSTOCK44/GETTY ©

Rooftop Bar

Shopping

Mall of the Emirates
MALL

13 🔒 Map p104, H5

This opulent mall is one of Dubai's best and busiest. Its excellent website has a day planner that allows you to create your personal mall itinerary so you can maximise your shopping time. There's a massive Virgin Megastore, an indoor ski resort and some excellent eateries. (www.malloftheemirates.com; Sheikh Zayed Rd)

Covent Garden Market
ARTS & CRAFTS

This weekend outdoor market handily located on the Walk at JBR (see **1** ◉ Map p104, B3) is as popular for a stroll along the lovely waterfront promenade (which is lined with cafes and restaurants that are great for people-watching) as it is for browsing through stalls of jewellery, art and crafts. Look out for hand-beaded Indian and Asian tops and shawls, Indian beaded slippers, and Jingerlilly's unusual handcrafted silver jewellery. (www.marinamarket.ae; The Walk at JBR, Dubai Marina; ⊙11am-7pm Fri & Sat Oct-Apr)

Marina Mall
MALL

14 🔒 Map p104, B4

A mall with around 160 stores where you won't get lost quite so readily as you will in those megamalls and yet where many of the shops are just as good. Here you can find such great stores as H&M, Reebok, Mango, Boots, Mothercare, Monsoon, Miss Sixty, the Early Learning Centre and the up-market UK supermarket chain Waitrose, as well as plenty of restaurants and cafes. (www.dubaimarinamall.com; Dubai Marina)

The Toy Store
TOYS

A mega toy store at the Mall of the Emirates (see **13** 🔒 Map p104, H5) with everything you need to entertain the wee ones, from life-size stuffed giraffes to toy telephones (mobiles, that is). Find it near the entrance to Ski Dubai. (Mall of the Emirates, Sheikh Zayed Rd)

Aminian Persian Carpets
CARPETS

This trusted rug trader at the Mall of the Emirates (see **13** 🔒 Map p104, H5) offers great service and stocks a wide selection of classic Persian carpets and

---

Ⓠ Local Life
Red Carpet Viewing

Splash out on an Emirati favourite: the Gold Class screening room at the **Vox Cinema** (Map p104, H5; www.voxcinemas.com; Mall of the Emirates, Sheikh Zayed Rd), complete with blankets, recliners, silver urns of popcorn and drinks in giant goblets. This is movie-watching for adults: no one under 18 years old is allowed, and everyone actually pays attention to the film. Buy tickets in advance through the website.

colourful tribal *kilims* (rugs). Plan to linger long: the collection is far more extensive than it first appears. (Mall of the Emirates, Sheikh Zayed Rd)

Harvey Nichols   DEPARTMENT STORE

The cool, contemporary design of Harvey Nic's – the largest outside the UK – and its discerning fashion coll-ections attract Dubai's fashionistas to the Mall of the Emirates (see **13** 🔒 Map p104, H5) in droves. The store's signature offerings – from a Personal Shopping Suite to exclusive concierge service Quintessentially – suit Dubai's VIP-loving shoppers to a tee. (www .harveynichols.com; Mall of the Emirates, Sheikh Zayed Rd)

Charles & Keith   FASHION

Singaporeans Charles and Keith Wong produce sassy, feminine, affordable shoes with fab attention to detail – pretty clogs with big cotton bows, strappy sandals with beading, sling-backs with buckles. The shop, at the Mall of the Emirates (see **13** 🔒 Map p104, H5), has summery, open styles perfect for Dubai's year-round sunshine and stifling heat. (www.charleskeith.com; Mall of the Emirates, Sheikh Zayed Rd)

Aizone   FASHION

You can lose yourself for hours in this enormous Lebanese fashion emporium

✅ Top Tip

Bargain Time

If you are visiting Dubai just after its two big shopping festivals (at the end of August or March), then you may still find seriously slashed prices in the shops, particularly at the Mall of the Emirates. The sales racks will probably be concealed at the back of the shop, so do ask – it's well worth it, as you could save up to 80% off the original price.

at the Mall of the Emirates (see **13** 🔒 Map p104, H5). Room after room are hung with hip, hard-to-find fashion from American Retro, Plenty, Bibelot, Citi-zens of Humanity, Lotus and Da-Nang, plus many more. A fashionista's heaven. (Mall of the Emirates, Sheikh Zayed Rd)

Camper   FASHION

The opening of Dubai's first Camper store at the Mall of the Emirates (see **13** 🔒 Map p104, H5) meant local hipsters no longer had to travel all the way to Barcelona (or Paris, Rome, New York, London...) for these funky, functional leather shoes and sneakers – crafted with centuries-old shoe-making techniques – although it was a good excuse while it lasted. (Mall of the Emirates, Sheikh Zayed Rd)

Top Sights
Abu Dhabi

Getting There

🚌 **Bus** Every 40 minutes from Dubai's Al Ghubaiba station (single/return Dh20/40, two hours one way).

🚕 **Taxi** A private taxi will cost around Dh250; sharing will reduce the price to around Dh50.

The emirate of Abu Dhabi has recently been investing heavily in culture, education and environmental innovation, with projects like the ambitious Saadiyat Island, which comes with four museums and a performing arts centre. One of the most obvious recent developments is the expansion and extension of the waterfront Corniche, with its white sandy beaches and broad Med-style promenade where you can rent a sunbed and brolly. But Abu Dhabi offers far more than a stretch of sand; try and visit for a day (or more) if you can.

Sheikh Zayed bin Sultan al-Nahyan Mosque

Don't Miss

Grand Mosque

The **Sheikh Zayed bin Sultan al-Nahyan Mosque** (Map p121; cnr Airport Rd & 5th St; admission free; ☺9am-noon Sat-Thu) is Abu Dhabi's stunning landmark, easily visible from afar and impressive inside and out. It can accommodate up to 40,000 worshippers in its central courtyard and main prayer hall. This snow-white house of worship has exquisite decorative detail with marble, gold, semiprecious stones, crystals and ceramics, and the world's largest Persian carpet.

Emirates Palace

You don't have to check in to check out the truly luxurious **Emirates Palace** (www.emiratespalace.com; Corniche Rd West), a striking landmark 3km to the west of the centre. It is colossal with 114 domes and lavish use of marble, gold and crystal throughout. Don't miss the lobby ATM machine – which spews out gold bars instead of common cash – or indulging in a cappuccino dusted with pure gold rather than chocolate.

Abu Dhabi Heritage Village

Located next to the flagpole on Breakwater, the **Heritage Village** (Map p121; Breakwater; admission free; ☺9am-1pm & 5-9pm Sat-Thu, 5-9pm Fri; 🚹) offers a glimpse of life in the pre-oil days with a re-creation of a souq, a traditional mosque, a Bedouin encampment with goat-hair tents and a typical desert *barasti* (palm-leaf house). Watch craftspeople making pots, blowing glass, beating brass and weaving on traditional looms. Don't miss the small museum here, as well. Unabashedly geared towards tourists, the 'village' is nonetheless entertaining.

☑ **Top Tips**

▸ Cruise along the Corniche via rented bike.

▸ In town, consider the hop-on, hop-off sightseeing bus to get around.

▸ Take a guided tour of the Grand Mosque, which includes a Q&A session (in English).

▸ Check www.yasisland.ae for the current concert star billing.

✖ **Take a Break**

If you are feeling peckish, you can't go wrong at urban chic **Jones the Grocer** (Map p121; ground fl, Pearl Plaza Tower, 32nd St; mains Dh50-62; ☺8am-10.30pm Sat-Thu, 9am-10.30pm Fri); its eclectic menu has an organic emphasis.

Another good choice is **Shakespeare & Co** (Map p121; ground fl, Central Market; mains Dh30-55; ☺7am-1am), particularly recommended for its bumper breakfast and filled crêpes.

Central Market

This inviting small **mall** (Map p121; www.centralmarket.ae; Hamdan St; 10am-10pm Sun-Thu, to 11pm Fri-Sat) on the site of the original main souq has been aesthetically designed with warm lattice woodwork. There are plenty of enticing stores here, including the Persian Carpet House & Antiques, Kashmir Cottage and the Chocolate Factory, plus restaurants and bars for that all-important taking-a-retail-break time.

Women's Handicraft Centre

If you have an interest in traditional crafts, swing by the government-run **Women's Handicraft Centre** (Al-Karamah St, Al Mushrif; admission free; 8.30am-1pm Sat-Wed) 4km south of the city centre. The main reason to visit is to see the workshops where local women demonstrate such crafts as *saddu* (carpet weaving), *talli* (embroidering), basket weaving, palm tree–frond weaving and henna application. There's also a small exhibit of costumes, textiles, camel bags and crafts, as well as a shop.

Nearby: Ferrari World Abu Dhabi

Ferrari World (www.ferrariworldabudhabi.com; Yas Island; adult/child Dh225/165; 11am-8pm Tue-Sun;) is a must-do for Ferrari fans or anyone fancying a ride on the world's fastest roller coaster (top speed: 200km/h). Other attractions include a Ferrari carousel for tots, a 4D movie theatre and an exhib-

---

Understand
Masdar City

Abu Dhabi has the Gulf's most ambitious environmental project taking shape. When completed (projected to be 2016), Masdar City will be the world's first carbon-neutral, zero-waste community powered entirely by renewable energy. The firm of British starchitect Norman Foster is providing the blueprint for what will be, essentially, a living laboratory for around 50,000 people. The brainpower is being supplied by the professors and students of the Masdar Institute of Science & Technology (MIST), in partnership with the renowned Boston-based Massachusetts Institute of Technology (MIT).

So what will life be like in Masdar City? For one, there won't be any cars, as people will commute by electric light-rail. Solar heat will be the main energy source, and thermal tubes will be integrated into building walls to provide hot water. It's a bold project aimed at achieving a cleaner future for a nation that derives its wealth from oil and currently ranks at the top of the world's per-capita energy consumption.

Masdar City is located approximately 23km south of the centre; check www.masdar.ae for more info.

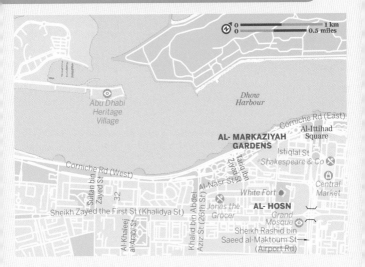

ition about the history of Ferrari. And, naturally, you can buy all that flaming red Ferrari gear here as well, ranging from hoodies to caps. Situated around 29km south of the centre, via Sheikh Rashid bin Saeed al-Maktoum St.

Nearby: Emirates National Auto Museum
A hangar-size ode to the automobile, this **museum** (www.enam.ae; Hanim Rd, off E11; admission free; ⏰ 7am-5pm; 🚼) is a treat even for those who can't tell a piston from a carburettor. Some 45km south of Abu Dhabi, on a lonely road towards the Liwa Oasis, the pyramid-shaped museum is home to an eclectic collection of 250 vehicles, from

concept cars to American classics – the oldest being a steam-powered Mercedes from 1885. Fascinating!

Nearby: Camel Racing
Camel racing is big business in the United Arab Emirates (UAE) and there are numerous tracks where these great desert athletes go nose to nose. **Al-Wathba Race Track** (☎ 02-583 9200; admission free) is located around 45km east of town off the E22 towards Al-Ain. Racing season runs from October to April, with meets usually held on Thursday and Friday from about 6.30am to 9am and then again between 2pm and 4pm.

Local Life
Sharjah's Charms & Culture

Getting There

🚌 **Bus** Buses to Al-Jubail station depart every 10 minutes from Al-Ittihad station in Deira and from Al Ghubaiba station in Bur Dubai. The ride takes about 40 minutes and costs just Dh5.

Sharjah has a far cheaper cost of living than Dubai, and is home to a large percentage of workers who commute daily to jobs all over the city. It is virtually just up the road, easily accessible and well worth a visit – not least for its wealth of cultural sights and its atmospheric souqs.

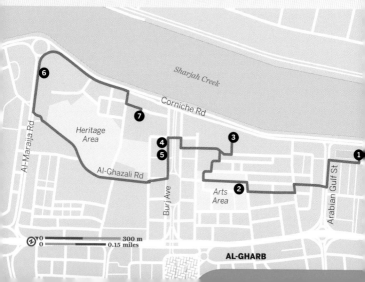

❶ Sharjah Museum of Islamic Civilisation

This fantastic **museum** (www.islamic museum.ae; cnr Corniche & Gulf Rds; admission Dh5; ⏰8am-8pm Sat-Thu, 4-8pm Fri) is a short stroll north of the centre. The collection covers various aspects of the Islamic faith, scientific accomplishments in the Arab world and 1400 years of Islamic art. Don't miss the central dome with its striking deep-blue zodiac mosaic.

❷ Sharjah Art Museum

The **Sharjah Art Museum** (www.sharjah museums.ae; ⏰8am-8pm Sat-Thu, 4-8pm Fri) is one of the United Arab Emirate's (UAE's) largest and most impressive galleries, and the organiser of the Sharjah Biennial (www.sharjahbiennial.org). The permanent exhibition includes 18th- and 19th-century oil paintings, watercolours and lithographs; curators also mount changing shows of local and international contemporary talent.

❸ ... Still More Art

Nearby **Bait Obaid al-Shamsi** (Corniche; ⏰9am-1pm & 4-8pm Sat-Thu) is a restored Creekside house honeycombed by artists' studios. You can chat with the artists and admire their latest works. Also here are the **Very Special Arts Centre**, a workshop and gallery for artists with disabilities, and the **Emirates Fine Arts Society**, which displays the work of local artists.

❹ Heritage Area

A short stroll along the creek brings you to Sharjah's Heritage Area. Many of the beautiful residences have been authentically restored using traditional materials such as sea rock, coral and gypsum. Wander through this labyrinthine quarter and you'll come upon the **Sharjah Heritage Museum** (Burj Ave; admission Dh5; ⏰8am-8pm Sat-Thu, 4-8pm Fri) with exhibits concentrating on local customs, traditions and arts and crafts, pre-oil days.

❺ Souqs & Sustenance

Next check out the atmospheric **Souq al-Arsa** (Burj Ave; ⏰9am-1pm & 4-9pm Sat-Thu, 4-9pm Fri), the oldest souq in the UAE. Head for the central courtyard for the best stores, selling everything from Indian pashminas to Yemeni daggers and at bargain prices – especially compared with Dubai. Seek out the traditional coffeehouse for a reviving mint tea and plate of dates.

❻ Go Persian

Nearby **Sadaf** (Al-Maraija Rd; mains Dh25-40) serves up excellent and authentic Persian cuisine. The spicy moist kebabs are particularly good, as is the 'Zereshk Polo Meat' (rice with Iranian red barberries and chicken or lamb). This place is really popular with Emirati families who dine in private booths.

❼ School Time

Now it's time to go to school. The **Al-Eslah School Museum** (admission Dh5; ⏰8am-8pm Sat-Thu, 4-8pm Fri) dates from 1935, when it welcomed students from all over the Gulf region. Recreated as it was then, with wooden desks and an upstairs dormitory, highlights include the headmaster's study with a Holy Quran made from palm wood.

The Best of
Dubai

Dubai's Best Walks

Dubai's Best...

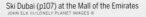

Ski Dubai (p107) at the Mall of the Emirates
JOHN ELK III/LONELY PLANET IMAGES ©

Best Walks
Deira Souq Stroll

🏃 The Walk

The Deira souq area is one of the most historic and atmospheric districts in Dubai and is best explored by foot, not least because parking is limited, driving is fraught (narrow roads, too much traffic...), and hops by taxi may mean you miss out on some of the best bits.

Start Spice Souq; Ⓜ Palm Deira (Green Line)

Finish Deira Covered Souq; Ⓜ Baniyas Sq (Green Line)

Length 2km/approximately three hours

🍴 Take a Break

If you've worked up an appetite rambling though Deira's souqs, a carnivorous feast at the **Afghan Khorasan Kebab House** (off Deira St; mains Dh15-35; 🕐 11am-1am) will help. Find it by turning right into an alley about half a block past the Naif Mosque. There are plenty of inexpensive cafes around the mosques, great for freshly squeezed fruit juices.

Spice Souq

❶ Spice Souq

As soon as you step off the *abra* (water taxi) at Deira Old Souq Abra Station, the heady scents of sumac, cinnamon, cloves and other spices will lure you to the tantalising **Spice Souq** (p29). The guttural singsong of Arabic bounces around the lanes of this small covered market as stall-holders unload aromatic and exotic herbs and spices.

❷ Heritage House

Heading towards the **Heritage House** (p28), you will pass stores selling nuts, pulses and rice. The shops belong to wholesalers who trade mainly with Iran, and use dhows to ply their goods. This is a good area to seek out saffron, pistachios (and other nuts) and Indian and Middle Eastern spices. Most shop owners will sell you a reasonable household quantity at more than reasonable wholesale prices.

❸ School Time

Chances are it is late morning by now – a hot

time of day – so head next door and explore another of Deira's fascinating historic-building museums: the **Al-Ahmadiya School** (p28). Teachers, in particular, may be interested in the informative videos about the development of United Arab Emirates (UAE) education.

❹ Gold Souq

Continue along Al-Ahmadiya St, turning right into Old Baladiya St, which has more wholesalers – this time trading in *gutras* (the white head cloth worn by men in the Gulf States) and *agals* (black head ropes used to secure a *gutra*), sandals and Chinese products. If you're in the market for an Emirati national dress as a souvenir, here's the place to shop. Ahead, to the left, is the wooden latticed entrance to the famous **Gold Souq** (p24).

❺ Deira Covered Souq

Exit the Gold Souq and follow Sikkat al-Khail St to Al-Soor St and turn right. This is the heart of the **Perfume Souq** (p28), a string of shops selling heady Arabian *attars* (perfumes) and *oud* (fragrant wood). Backtrack and continue straight on 107 St, which flanks the **Deira Covered Souq** (p28). It can be bedlam here – and super-atmospheric, with hawkers competing noisily for trade, and thus a fitting place to end your Deira souq stroll.

Best Walks
Waterside Walk

🏃 The Walk

This heritage walk of Dubai's oldest area kicks off, appropriately, in the historic Bastakia Quarter, where you can wander around the atmospheric narrow lanes and peek into the renovated wind-tower houses. It covers several of Dubai's most interesting traditional sights and provides an insight into the Dubai of yesteryear, with not a shopping mall, skyscraper or ski slope in sight.

Start Al Serkal Cultural Foundation

Finish Heritage & Diving Villages

Length 3km/three to four hours

🍴 Take a Break

With excellent views of the Creek, **Blue Barjeel** (snacks Dh 12-15) serves Lebanese cuisine, like falafel and hummus, along with a range of fruit juices and teas. It's around 50m west of the restaurant Bait Al Wakeel (p48).

Bastakia Quarter (p44)

❶ Cultural Foundation

Check out the lavishly decorated **Bastakiah Nights**, a touristy Middle Eastern restaurant in a traditional courtyard house. Ask if you can have a look around or kick-start your day with an energising coffee. Move on to the nearby **Al Serkal Cultural Foundation** (p46), an art gallery and cultural centre within yet another charming courtyard building.

❷ Al-Fahadi Roundabout

Enjoy the exquisite jewellery, ceramics, paintings, illustrated books and souvenirs at the gift shop of the **Basta Art Cafe** (p48). Cool down with a fruit juice here, then duck into next door's **Majlis Gallery** (p46) to see the artwork. Continue north along bustling Al-Fahidi St.

❸ Silk Wonders

Don't miss the tempting selection of stores at **Silk Wonders**. The souqlike complex sells inexpensive clothes, shawls and accessories from India and Iran. It's also good for gift T-shirts, sequinned bedspreads and silk-and-wool rugs to blitz your luggage allowance.

❹ Dubai Museum

Duck out of the heat and explore the fascinating **Dubai Museum** (p40). Take a look at the mutidomed Grand Mosque across the way, and if you're interested in watches and gold jewellery, check out the small stores north of the nearby Arabian Courtyard Hotel.

❺ Creekside Plaza

Take the lane along the mosque's right-hand side, passing the Hindu temples on colourful **Hindi Lane** (p44). Follow this to the end, then turn right down a walkway leading to **Creekside Plaza**, which has picture-perfect views of the *abra* and dhow traffic, as well as the restored wind towers across the water in Deira.

❻ Shindagha Heritage Area

Stroll beneath the wooden arcades of the **Bur Dubai Souq** (p44), walk past the boats at the Bur Dubai Abra Station, and continue along the waterfront to the **Shindagha Heritage Area**. Stop at the **Traditional Architecture Museum** (p46) and the **Sheikh Saeed al-Maktoum House** (p46), and make a final stop at the **Heritage & Diving Villages** (p44).

Best
Eating

Dubai has some of the best restaurants in the UAE. Dining out is a major pastime of locals, residents and visitors, and the restaurant scene has never been as varied and exciting as it is right now. The sheer number of restaurants – and types of cuisine – is huge. In short, if you enjoy food, you will love Dubai.

Celebrity Chefs

It's pretty hard to find anywhere on a par with Dubai when it comes to the number of celebrity chefs bubbling away in the gourmet culinary cauldron. And although one or two have departed (most notably Gordon Ramsay), new names include everyone's kitchen-sink darling, Jamie Oliver.

Vegetarian Dining

Dubai is good for vegetarians. Many of the Indian restaurants are vegetarian and you can also fill up fast with Lebanese all-veg mezzes. Thai places offer chilli-spiced veg curries and soups.

Wining & Dining

If you enjoy a glass of wine with dinner, then you will learn fast that this is not standard practice in Dubai. There are essentially two types of restaurant here: the hotel restaurant and the independent. Only hotels are licensed to serve alcohol, which is why they house the city's most popular dining rooms.

OLAF FEY/CORBIS ©

☑ Top Tips

▶ Most restaurants are open seven days a week.

▶ Make reservations for hotel restaurants, be prepared to give your mobile number and expect a call if you're late.

▶ Make weekend bookings for top tables, including Friday brunch, at least a week ahead.

Best Cheap Eats

Xiao Wei Yang (p30) A genuine hotpot restaurant with wonderfully fresh ingredients and spicy condiments.

Noodle House (p91) Basic decor, but tasty Asian food with noodle

Outdoor restaurants along Dubai Creek

dishes, dumplings, pancakes, and oodles more...

Ravi (p62) This is where in-the-know Pakistanis eat. Enough said.

Best Gourmet Experiences

Rhodes Mezzanine (p109) Specialises in innovative takes on classic British dishes.

Traiteur (p30) Come here for superb French food and an elegant, romantic ambience.

Eauzone (p110) Waterfront location, excellent international cuisine (and the best puddings in the UAE!).

Shabestan (p31) Superb Persian cuisine in an elegant atmosphere. Dress the part.

Best For Steaks

Fire & Ice (p48) Raffles' sophisticated steakhouse exudes a New York vibe.

Tribes (p111) African-themed restaurant with hearty meat dishes.

The Meat Company (p72) Great canal views, quality steaks, plus some veggie sides.

Best for Foodie Treats

Bateel (p55) The place for deliciously fancy and succulent dates.

Organic Foods & Cafe (p94) A rare place specialising in organic foods, including plenty of gourmet goodies.

Candylicious (p94) Every candy and chocolate brand you could possibly think of.

Lime Tree Cafe (p62) The best carrot cake in town, and the brownies are pretty irresistible too.

Best for Atmosphere

Asha's (p48) Warm tandoori colours, sultry fusion music and heart-warming cuisine at this top Indian restaurant.

Emporio Armani Caffé (p90) A seriously classy Italian-style cafe surrounded by designer boutiques.

Ivy (p89) Soak up the classic British atmosphere at this celebrated restaurant.

Baker & Spice (p90) Grab a table on the terrace overlooking the Dubai Fountain.

Best
Bars

Dubai is a cosmopolitan city, and its bars are as cool as they come, fusing exotic styles in their drinks, designs and music. The best nights are Thursday and Friday, when expats burn off steam from their 60-hour work weeks. Hotels that are licensed to serve alcohol are home to most of the best bars.

The Sin Tax

How exactly do the authorities decide on those sky-high booze prices? Yes, it's all down to a hefty haram (literally 'forbidden') tax. And prices aren't going to come down any time soon: a duopoly controls all the alcohol sales in Dubai. If drinking is important to you, buy your alcohol at Dubai Duty Free before leaving the airport.

Sheesha Cafes

If you're not up for drinking, hit the mellow *sheesha* (water pipe used to smoke tobacco) cafes and play a game of backgammon. Emiratis don't like to be around alcohol, but they sure love coffee. Dubai's *sheesha* cafes also provide great insight into local culture. Even if you don't smoke, it's worth reclining languorously and sampling a puff to better understand this traditional pastime.

Ordering Drinks

Alcohol is expensive, but that doesn't stop rowdy Westerners from downing pint after shot after pint. Nurse your drinks or you'll shell out a lot of dirhams. Long waits at the bar are common at crowded venues. Conversely, waiters are trained to upsell guests so make clear exactly who at the table wants another drink or you may wind up with a hefty bill.

TYPHOONSKI/DREAMSTIME.COM ©

☑ Top Tips

▶ Alcohol service is illegal between 4pm and 6pm on Friday and Saturday.

▶ Dubai has zero-tolerance laws on drink driving. Even one glass of alcohol can see you prosecuted, or even imprisoned.

▶ Being drunk in public is equally unacceptable and severely punished.

Best Sea Breezes

Maya (p113) A fabulously situated rooftop bar for enjoying the sunset over the sea.

Rooftop Bar (p114) Sophisticated, luxurious open-air bar with

Vu's Bar, designed by architect Hazel WS Wong

twinkling lanterns and starry views.

Bahri Bar (p74) Romantic location overlooking the canals at Madinat Jumeirah with the Burj al-Arab backdrop.

Best Vistas

Neos (p94) Another high-in-the-sky bar with striking art deco furnishings and killer cocktails.

QDs (p33) Overlooking the Creek and specialising in champagne and *sheesha*: a bewitching combination.

360° (p74) This elegant bar enjoys a fabulous position overlooking the iconic Burj al-Arab.

Best For Buzzy Atmosphere

Buddha Bar (p113) The sexy lighting and exotic decor attract the who's-who brigade.

People by Crystal (p52) One of the most popular bars and clubs for a glammed-up local crowd.

Barasti Bar (p113) Expats' favourite: an informal, lively and refreshingly unpretentious bar by the beach.

Malecon (p64) The place to come to show off those hip-swinging salsa steps.

Best Champagne Bars

Bar 44 (p112) Attracting a glamorous crowd of young sophisticates

with its great views and elegant atmosphere.

Cin Cin's (p94) Fabulous champagnes, good wines by the glass and a cigar lounge.

Vu's Bar (p95) Stylish setting, stunning views and an impressive range of champagnes and cocktails – plus oysters.

Best for Special Promotions

Barasti Bar (p113) This lively informal bar has regular theme nights, promotions and deals on drinks.

Left Bank (p75) Ladies' night is Wednesday, with cut-price cocktails.

The Terrace (p33) Sunday is ladies' night; on Monday there are drinks specials for all.

Best
Shopping

Dubai loves to shop. The city has just about per-fected the art of the mall, which is the de facto air-conditioned 'town plaza'. Dubai malls have ski slopes, ice rinks and aquariums. They look like ancient Persia, futuristic movie sets or a little bit of Disneyland – surrounded by desert.

YOLINDO DE KOCK/DREAMSTIME.COM ©

How to Find a Bargain

The range of stores – high-street to designer, elec-tronics to carpets – is amazing, but true bargains are rare outside of the annual Dubai Shopping Fes-tival in January. The souqs in Deira and Bur Dubai can have good prices, providing you're willing to haggle. Deira's Gold Souq is one of the cheapest places in the world to buy gold.

The Shopping Ritual

Shopping is a daily ritual for Emiratis, but in Dubai it is taken to a sublime level. Elegant local women, designer *shaylas* (black veils or head-scarves) dripping with Swarovski crystals, treat a trip to Saks the way their burka-wearing mothers might a morning at the spice souq. They take their time, make their choice, scrutinise the product, then, when they're ready to buy, ask for a discount. Do the same.

Bedouin Jewellery

Bedouin jewellery is brilliant in Dubai, and with the steady popularity of boho ethnic chic, makes a great gift. Look for elaborate silver necklaces and pendants, chunky earrings and rings, and wedding belts, many of which incorporate coral, turquoise and semiprecious stones. Very little of the older Bedouin jewellery comes from the Emirates; most of it originates in Oman, Yemen and Afghanistan.

☑ **Top Tips**

▶ Fragrant Iranian and Spanish saffron costs far less here than it does back home.

▶ Try before you buy and ask about return policies, es-pecially for gifts.

Best Shopping Malls

Dubai Mall (p82) This extraordinary shopping mall, entertainment cen-tre and restaurant hub is the largest in the world.

Mall of the Emirates (p116) Home of another one-off wonder: Ski Dubai.

BurJuman Centre (p54) A mall of a more manageable size, with quality shops, good restaurants and a con-venient metro stop.

Dubai Mall

Deira City Centre (p35) A no-nonsense shopping mall with a sound mix of international chains and smaller independent stores.

Best for Exciting Fashions

If (p79) Exciting cutting-edge fashion by up-and-coming young designers.

S*uce (p64) Innovative fashions with funky colours and designs.

Harvey Nichols (p117) Supercool, super-contemporary and superclassy fashions for gals looking for that stylish edge.

Best for Souvenirs

Al-Orooba Oriental (p55) Great for Bedouin jewellery, ceramics, prayer beads and woven carpets and rugs.

Lata's (p77) Some of the best choices of souvenirs, including the unabashedly kitsch, and quality handicrafts.

O' de Rose (p78) The place to come for quirky and unusual gifts.

Best for Accessories

Covent Garden Market (p116) Several stores here sell accessories, including handmade jewellery, sequinned bags and colourful scarves.

Blue Cactus (p65) The brightly coloured jewellery and accessories here come primarily from Mexico, which gives them an original edge.

Best
Beaches

Dubai's locals love their beaches. While Jumeirah residents living within splashing distance of the crystal-clear turquoise waters make it a daily ritual to head down to the beach, the rest of Dubai makes an effort to hit the beach on weekends. Dubai's verdant beach parks are also popular, as much for family barbecues as for swimming and sunbathing opportunities.

REINHARD SCHMID/4CORNERS ©

Facilities & Activities

Overall, Dubai's beaches are clean and those with an entry fee are patrolled by lifeguards. The facilities (change room, kiosks and children's playgrounds) are excellent. Although the Palm Island developments have blotted the horizon and sometimes cause sediment to cloud the normally clear water, the beach resorts along the Jumeirah stretch are some of the best in the world, with enormous swimming pools, wet bars, palm-filled gardens, and excellent water sports and activities. Fortunately, you don't have to stay at a hotel to enjoy Dubai's beaches, as many resorts run beach clubs with daily and weekly access.

Best Free Beaches

Kite Beach (p72) A delightful stretch of sand, popular with kitesurfers, but with no facilities.

Umm Suqeim Beach (p72) Pristine white-sand beach with stunning views of the Burj al-Arab and good facilities.

Jumeirah Open Beach (p62) Paralleled by a paved path popular with strollers, joggers, inline skaters and cyclists. Some facilities.

Best Beach Resorts

One&Only Royal Mirage (http://royalmirage .oneandonlyresorts.com) Kilometre-long private beach and water sports, including windsurfing, sailing and kayaking.

Jumeirah Beach Hotel (www.jumeirahbeachhotel .com) Minimum one-week membership provides access to private beach, pools, tennis courts, PADI dive centre and kids' resort.

Mina A'Salam & Al-Qasr (www.jumeirah.com /en/hotels-and-resorts /destinations/dubai /madinat-jumeirah) The daily pass gives you access to a dreamy beach and fabulous pools, and includes a food voucher.

Best
Souqs

In contrast to the sleek, shiny, squeaky-clean shopping malls, the cacophony, colour and chaos of the souqs is what makes them so appealing. Neither the breezy wooden arcade of the Bur Dubai Souq nor the ramshackle market shops in Deira resemble the palm-roofed bazaars of the 1830s, but today's souqs remain full of character and are among the best in the Gulf region.

REINHARD SCHMID/4CORNERS ©

☑ **Top Tip**

▶ Don't forget to shop around in the souq: it's unlikely that the item you are after is a one-off.

Bargaining

Be sure to bargain in the souqs. It is expected. Start by halving the price quoted and expect to pay around 75% of what was originally offered. Always carry cash as cards are often not accepted. The faux-Arabian souqs, such as Souq Al-Bahar, are generally more expensive and are less likely to drop prices as much, due to expensive overheads.

Souq Categories

There are essentially two styles of souq: the bustling, noisy and crowded street souqs in Deira and Bur Dubai and the more sanitised variety, usually attached to malls and hotels, which are generally air-conditioned and highly decorative, with lots of elaborate architectural detail.

Best 'Faux' Souqs

Souq al-Bahar (p88) This souq has a stunning setting overlooking the Dubai Fountain and Burj Khalifa.

Souq Madinat Jumeirah (p68) Ideally situated on Madinat's canals, with upmarket souvenir shops and superb restaurants.

Khan Murjan Souq (p54) The ornate design here is impressive, as is the range of stores.

Best Souqs

Gold Souq (p24) A glittering market of gold. Don't miss it.

Deira Spice Souq (p29) A tantalising, atmospheric souq selling herbs and spices.

Bur Dubai Souq (p44) This rambling souq specialises in wonderful textiles.

Best
Architecture

Contrasting with Dubai's shiny modern towers is the equally compelling Bastakia Quarter, with its traditional wind-tower buildings. The blend of typical Arabian architecture with futuristic structures is a remarkable sight, while, interestingly, much of the city's recent architecture sees a return to traditional Arabian forms.

SPREEPHOTO.DE/GETTY ©

Traditional Architecture

There were two types of traditional house here – the *masayf*, a summer house incorporating a wind tower, and the *mashait*, a winter house with a courtyard. Other traditional architectural styles are religious (mosques), defensive (forts) and commercial (souqs).

Environmental Impact

In contrast to traditional architecture, which was all about function over form and built with regard to the environment, modern architecture in Dubai (until recently) has embraced an 'anything goes' ethos that disregards the climate. About 90% of the buildings use concrete, steel and glass, which are not best suited to Dubai's extreme heat.

Best Heritage Architecture

Sheikh Saeed al-Maktoum House & Traditional Architecture Museum (p46) Aesthetically restored, the magnificent court yard houses here have been turned into museums.

Bastakia Quarter (p44) This historic quarter is home to traditional houses built nearly a century ago.

Heritage House & Al-Ahmadiya (p28) These two modest museums still reflect their traditional architectural roots.

☑ **Top Tip**

▶ You must reserve in advance to visit either of Dubai's Burj buildings.

Best Iconic Architecture

Burj al-Arab (p72) A 60-floor, sail-shaped super-luxurious hotel built on an artificial island.

Burj Khalifa (p88) The world's tallest building clocks in at a cloud-tickling 828m.

Jumeirah Beach Hotel (www.jumeirahbeachhotel .com) This long S-shaped construction represents a wave, with the Gulf as its backdrop.

Best
Spas

A weekly pampering is an essential part of life for many expats, and an increasing number of visitors to Dubai are adding a spa treatment to their 'to-do' list (right after the suntan and shopping). There are tranquil, minimalist spas and exotic Moroccan- and Turkish-style hammams, but what Dubai does best is the extravagant luxury spa, with ornate pillars, gold leaf and big sunken baths.

Typical Treatments

Most spas have a long menu of classic treatments, ranging from facials, exfoliations, scrubs, soaks, wraps and massages to the much-hyped hot-oil ayurvedic therapies. Others are more innovative and very in tune with the lifestyle (jet lag recovery treatment, anyone?) and culture (yes, we'll take the Cleopatra recipe milk bath please).

Themed Packages

These are the most fun treatments and usually include a combination scrub, bath, massage and facial, along with the use of the steam room and wet area, herbal teas, juices and a healthy lunch. They range from 90-minute treatments to a more indulgent full day at the spa.

Best Spas

Talise (p96) Some unusual revitalising treatments, including flotation pools, in mellow surrounds.

One&Only Spa (p106) Twelve sumptuous private rooms for holistic and personally tailored treatments.

Softtouch Spa (p109) Handily located next to the ski slopes, it has soothing Asian-style decor and luxurious treatments.

Best Spa Treatments

Oxygen Lounge (p96) Breathe deeply and revitalise those capillaries post-flight by indulging in an Oxygen Lounge session at Talise.

Oriental Hammam (p106) A wonderful quasi-Moroccan bathhouse at the One&Only Spa for an ultra-self-pampering experience.

Dead Sea Salt Bath (p35) Luxuriate in a soothing and revitalising salt bath, followed by an ayurvedic massage at Amara.

Best
For Kids

Arab culture reveres children, and Dubai has plenty of kiddie entertainment, much of it extravagant in novelty value (but not necessarily in cost). Water parks are an obvious choice, while hotel pools and beaches offer tamer splashing scope. Older children can enjoy any number of adrenalin-fuelled activities, and there's plenty of free stuff for youngsters, as well.

PHILIP & KAREN SMITH/LONELY PLANET IMAGES ©

Junior Foodies

When spirits and feet start to drag, there's plenty of ice cream and kid-friendly meals to pick them back up. If you're not sure where to eat, mall food courts are a sure bet. All hotels also have at least one restaurant suitable for families (usually the buffet). In short, fear not: your hardest task will be strapping the kids into the taxi, not finding something to eat.

Playgrounds & Parks

Though you won't want to visit them during the serious sunburn season of July and August, Dubai has a handful of parks with picnic areas and playgrounds for children to let off steam. One of the biggest and best for activities is **Za'abeel Park** (p47), with great sports facilities, plus a lake.

Keeping the Teens Happy

Okay, so they've done the ski slopes, disco-danced at the ice rink, splashed around at the water parks and enjoyed a fashionable strut around the malls. Is there more to prevent teens from succumbing to total Facebook-deprivation meltdown? Fortunately, yes! Consider sand-boarding, camel-riding, an overnight desert safari or even a trekking trip to the Hajar mountains. All are available with local tour companies.

☑ Top Tips

▶ For general advice, see Lonely Planet's *Travel with Children*.

▶ Peekaboo (www .peekaboo.ae) has crèches/play centres for children under seven at several shopping malls.

▶ Children under five travel free on public transport.

Best Water Parks

Aquaventure (p106) One of the largest water parks in the world (but you knew that), with rides suitable for all the family.

Wild Wadi Waterpark (p76) The original family-favourite waterpark, catering to every age with gentle pools and kamikaze slides.

Aquaventure

Best Themed Attractions

KidZania (p97) This interactive miniature city offers the ultimate in role-play options.

Sega Republic (p97) Older kids can head for this indoor game park with themed areas and motion-simulator rides.

Stargate (p47) Space cadets can go starry eyed at the space-themed amusement park in Za'abeel Park.

Best for Nature Lovers

Aquarium & Underwater Zoo (p82) Kids will be fascinated by the underwater and animal worlds here.

Lost Chambers (p106) More of the same at this labyrinth of underwater tanks and fish-filled tunnels.

Dolphin Bay (p106) Children can get up close and personal with dolphins here.

Ras Al-Khor Wildlife Sanctuary (p88) Junior twitchers can see flamingos and other exotic birds through binoculars.

Best for Chilled-Out Kids

Dubai Ice Rink (p96) Pint-sized kids can cool down big time with a trip to Dubai Mall's ice rink.

Ski Dubai (p107) For those who want to do the full alpine bit and tackle the snow slopes.

Best
Money Savers

There is no denying that Dubai can easily tempt you to part with loads of dirhams (the Gold Souq comes glitteringly to mind…). Fortunately, there is a freebie flipside. It's admittedly not that extensive, though, which is why we have included some cheapie options here, as well. For money-saving meals, see p130.

WALTER BIBIKOW/GETTY ©

Souq Time

Wandering around the souqs in Bur Dubai (p44) and Deira (p24 & p29) has to be one of the most enjoyable and insightful experiences here and, unless you succumb to the very persuasive vendors, it will cost you nothing more than shoe leather.

Peruse the Art

Don your sunhat and sunblock, shift into exploring mode and head for the industrial-zone confusion that is Al-Quoz (p84), home to many of Dubai's most exciting art galleries. Many of the galleries feature contemporary young artists from the Arab world; others have huge, big-name installations.

☑ **Top Tips**

▶ Take advantage of happy hour and special drink promotions offered by many bars.

▶ Hotel prices plummet up to 50% during July and August.

Best Free Museums

Traditional Architecture Museum (p46) Free and offers a fascinating glimpse of traditional Arab building techniques.

Heritage House (p28) Provides a peek at a wealthy pearl merchant's residence.

Sheikh Saeed Al-Maktoum House (pictured above; p46) An architectural gem treating history buffs to a jaunt back in time for just Dh2.

Al-Ahmadiya School (p28) Dates from 1912 and has dioramas of classrooms and Quran lessons.

Best Free Beaches

Jumeirah Open Beach (p62) A pleasant sandy strip flanked by a promenade.

Kite Beach (p72) A pristine beach popular with water-sports enthusiasts but with no facilities.

Umm Suqeim Beach (p72) In the shadow of the Burj al-Arab, another great beach – this time with top facilities.

Best
Clubbing

To meet the insatiable demands of Dubai's cool young clubbing population, an increasing number of international DJs are racking up frequent-flyer miles coming to Dubai. There's something on to suit all tastes every night of the week. Wednesdays through Fridays are the big nights out, but clubbers come out in force when big-name international DJs jet in for the weekend.

Types of Music

You will hear all types of music spinning on Dubai's turntables – R&B, soul, funk, hip hop, trance, tribal, electronica, drum and bass and house in their myriad incarnations. Fusions of Arab, African, Indian, Latino and Euro styles are also emerging. Serious clubbers should sign up to mailing lists before they leave home to find out what is playing where and to get hold of tickets – the best DJs sell out fast.

Best for DJs

Chi (p52) Top-ranking DJs play funk, house, disco, drum and bass and whatever else inspires.

People by Crystal (p52) Attracts top disc spinners and a glam crowd of party people.

Trilogy (p75) Superb smoochy atmosphere and some of the best DJs on the circuit.

Best for Atmosphere

Ku Bu (p33) A moodily lit atmospheric place with drapes, cool DJs and head-spinning cocktails.

360° (p74) Enjoy magical views of the Burj al-Arab along with a chatty-sophisticates vibe.

N'Dulge (p114) One of the sexiest clubs in Dubai, situated on the iconic Palm Jumeirah.

DARYL VISSCHER/GETTY ©

☑ Top Tip

▸ Some top clubs require advance reservations, especially if a top DJ is spinning the discs.

Best for Fancy Cocktails

Senyar (p114) This super-stylish bar pulls in the punters with its live music and glam ambience.

Bahri Bar (p74) Breath-taking views and sublime cocktails make this waterfront bar hard to beat.

Boudoir (p64) This place has a supersexy ambience and some superb colourful cocktails.

Best
Sports Events

Dubai's winter months are tailor-made for outdoor sporting pursuits, and the city obliges by holding an excellent roster of international events. The most social happening of Dubai's sporting calendar, the Dubai Rugby Sevens tournament, sees many of Dubai's expats worshipping another sport – that of drinking beer outdoors!

Camel Racing

Camel racing is not only a popular spectator sport but deeply rooted in the Emirati soul and originally practised only at weddings and special events. These days it's big business, with races held between October and early April at **Al-Lisaili Race Track** (📞04-338 8170), located past the Rugby Sevens stadium, and **Al-Wathba Race Track** (p121) in Abu Dhabi.

Best Sporting Events

Dubai World Cup (www.dubaiworldcup.com) Held annually in March; the culmination of the horse-racing season.

Dubai Tennis Championships (www.dubaitennischampionships.com) Attracts big-name players every February.

Dubai Desert Classic (www.dubaidesertclassic.com) Held every February, attracting the golfing elite.

Dubai Rugby Sevens (www.dubairugby7s.com) A three-day event in November or December.

Dubai Marathon (www.dubaimarathon.org) Thousands of runners turn up for this popular street race held annually in January.

Best Sporting Venues

Emirates Golf Club (www.dubaigolf.com) The first grass championship course in the Middle East with two 18-hole courses.

Meydan Racecourse (www.meydan.ae/racecourse) Futuristic stadium that can accommodate up to 60,000 spectators.

The Sevens Rugby Stadium (www.dubairugby7s.com) This superb purpose-built stadium is located around 30 minutes south of Sheikh Zayed Rd.

STEVE CRISPY/CORBIS ©

Survival Guide

Survival Guide

Before You Go

When to Go

°C/°F Temp
Rainfall inches/mm

→ Winter (Dec–Feb)
A good season to visit, although you can expect occasional cold patches around the New Year.

→ Spring (Mar–Apr)
One of the best times to be here, with temperatures around 30°C.

→ Summer (Jul–Aug)
Months to avoid, when temperatures average

around 43°C with a stifling 95% humidity. The one plus is that accommodation prices are slashed.

→ Autumn (Oct–Nov)
Together with springtime, this is an ideal period to visit as temperatures are tolerable.

Book Your Stay

☑ **Top Tip** If you like a drink, make sure your hotel isn't 'dry'!

→ There are essentially two types of hotel in Dubai: the beach resort and the city hotel.

→ Beach hotels are generally five star, with private beaches and luxurious facilities.

→ Midrange options cater to the business market, with meeting facilities, modern rooms and gyms.

→ Budget hotels vary considerably. Go for a respected name like Ibis.

→ Hotel apartments are another option and are particularly well suited to families.

→ Room rates fluctuate enormously; always ask for the 'best price'.

→ Most hotels are child-friendly, and facilities offered are of an extremely high standard.

Useful Websites

Lonely Planet Hotels
(www.hotels.lonelyplanet
.com) Lonely Planet's
online booking service,
with the lowdown on the
best places to stay.

HRS (www.hrs.com) Emphasis on budget hotels
and hotel apartments.

Definitely Dubai (www
.definitelydubai.com) Run
by the official tourist
authority, with a solid
choice of mainly mid-
range to top-end hotels.

Bed & Breakfast World
(www.bedandbreakfastworld
.com/dubai) More oriented
towards hotel apartments
and budget hotels than
traditional B&Bs.

Best Budget

Golden Sands Apart-
ments (www.goldensands
dubai.com) Well-equipped
apartments in Bur Dubai.

Centro Barsha (www
.rotana.com) Small
contemporary rooms a
10-minute walk from the
Mall of the Emirates.

Ibis Mall of the Emir-
ates (www.ibishotel.com)
Close to the World Trade
Centre, and part of a well-
known chain. Rooms are
compact but adequate.

Villa 47 (www.villa47.com) A
sweet B&B near the air-
port on a quiet residential
street.

Best Midrange

Riviera Hotel (www
.rivierahotel-dubai.com) A
reliable choice, with a
soothing colour scheme,
plush carpeting and great
Creek views.

Orient Guest House
(www.orientguesthouse
.com) Romantic small
guesthouse in the heart
of the historic Bastakia
Quarter.

Ramada Hotel (www
.ramadadubai.com) Along
with the fabulous stained
glass in the atrium,
rooms here get the
thumbs-up for their split-
level spaciousness.

Rydges Plaza (www.rydges
.com) Has a clubby

English-style decor:
classic wallpaper, plush
carpeting and shiny dark-
wood furniture.

Best Top End

One&Only Royal Mirage
(www.oneandonlyresorts
.com) This hotel is a class
act all round, with its
sumptuous Moorish-
inspired architecture and
top-notch facilities.

Al-Qasr (www.madinat
jumeirah.com) Styled after
an Arabian summer pal-
ace, rooms sport heavy
arabesque flourishes,
rich colours and cushy
furnishings.

Jumeirah Emirates
Tower (www.jumeirah.com)
Housed in one of Dubai's
soaring steel-and-glass
buildings, this is considered one of the Middle
East's top business
hotels.

Single or Sharing?

According to local culture, unmarried men and
women should not share a room. In practice
most hotels turn a blind eye. If this is something
that concerns you, reserve your hotel in advance
providing names in full. Having two different
names is no tip-off, as most married Arab
women keep their name. Two men sharing is
acceptable, while single women checking into a
hotel room alone may raise eyebrows due to the
large number of 'working girls' in town.

Raffles Dubai (www .dubai.raffles.com) Built in the shape of a pyramid, this high-octane hot spot sports magnificent oversize rooms.

Arriving in Dubai

☑ **Top Tip** For the best way to get to your accom- modation, see p17.

Dubai International Airport

Airport Buses

Buses (☎ 800 9090; Dh3) run every 30 minutes to Deira's Al-Sabkha Bus Station (bus 401; Map p26) and Al-Ghubaiba Bus Station in Bur Dubai (bus 402; Map p42).

Metro

The Dubai **Metro** (www. rta.ae) runs from Satur- day to Wednesday from 5.50am to midnight, Thursday 5.50am to 1am and Friday 1pm to 1am. The Red Line makes several stops in Deira, including Deira City Cen- tre (Map p26), Al-Rigga

(Map p26) and Union Sq (Map p26). Also convenient for hotels in downtown Dubai around the Financial Centre (Map p86), the Mall of the Emirates (Map p104) and Dubai Marina (Map p104), where a connecting feeder bus has several stops in the marina.

Change at Union for the Metro's Green Line for additional Deira and Bur Dubai stops, including Baniyas Sq (Map p26), Palm Deira (Map p26), Al-Ras (Map p26) and Al- Ghubaiba (Map p26).

Taxis

From the arrivals area, Dubai Transport taxis cost between Dh45 and Dh90 depending on your destination and include a Dh20 airport surcharge.

Getting Around

Boat

☑ **Best for**... scenic rides.

➡ *Abras* (traditional wooden boats; Dh1) are a wonderful way to cross the Creek. Water buses

Nol Cards

Before you hop on a local bus or the Metro, you must buy a rechargeable **Nol** (www.nol.ae) card from ticket offices at any metro station, most bus stations, or from ticket vending machines.

There are four categories of Nol Card: red, sil- ver, gold and blue (aimed at residents). If you're only going to use public transport a few times, get a Red Card, which costs Dh2 and may be recharged for up to 10 journeys. Fares depend on distance and are divided into zones.

Those planning on travelling more frequently should get a Silver Card for Dh20 (including Dh14 of credit). The Gold Card has the same features as the Silver Card but gives you access to the Gold Class carriage and is roughly double the price.

Day passes for unlimited travel in all zones are Dh14. Children under five years old travel free.

(Dh5) are also good for sightseeing.

Bus

☑ **Best for**... longer trips.

➡ A network of 79 bus routes covers most of Dubai. However, buses can be crowded and slow. Of more interest are the long-distance buses.

➡ Buses to Abu Dhabi (one-way/return Dh20/40, two hours, every 40 minutes) leave from Dubai's Al-Ghubaiba Bus Station (Map p42). The bus is comfortable.

➡ For more information, visit www.rta.ae.

Taxis

☑ **Best for**... convenience.

➡ Dubai has a large, modern fleet of metered taxis, but not enough to meet demand. Expect long waits, especially during peak hour and at shopping malls.

➡ The starting fare is Dh3 (Dh6 if you book), plus Dh1.60 per km.

➡ From 10pm to 6am starting fare is Dh3.50, plus Dh1.70 per km.

Metro

☑ **Best for**... price and speed.

➡ The Red Line runs from near Dubai International Airport to Jebel Ali (Dh5.80, one hour eight minutes, every five to eight minutes).

➡ The Green Line runs from Etislat, northwest of the airport, to Dubai Healthcare City (Map p42; Dh4.10, 45 minutes, every six to eight minutes), just south of Oud Metha in Bur Dubai.

➡ The advantages of the metro include low fares (Dh1.80 to Dh5.80) and frequency (every 10 minutes from 6am to 11pm Saturday to Thursday, and from 1pm to midnight on Fridays).

➡ A disadvantage is that you may still need to take a taxi from the end metro stop to your final destination.

➡ For more information, visit www.rta.ae.

Essential Information

....

Business Hours

☑ **Top Tip** Don't forget that hours are reduced during Ramadan.

Restaurants noon to 3pm and 7.30pm to midnight

Shopping malls 10am to 10pm Sunday to Wednesday, 10am to midnight Thursday to Saturday

Souqs 9am to 1pm and 4pm to 9pm Saturday to Thursday, 4pm to 9pm Friday

In this guide, times are not included unless they differ from the above.

Electricity

230V/50Hz

Emergency

Ambulance (📞998/999)

Fire department (📞997)

Police (emergency 📞999, headquarters 📞04-229 2222)

Money

☑ **Top Tip** Bring cash to the souqs as credit cards are not widely accepted.

UAE dirham (Dh) notes come in denominations of five, 10, 20, 50, 100, 200, 500 and 1000. There are Dh1, 50 fils, 25 fils, 10 fils and 5 fils coins.

ATMs

Most credit and debit cards can be used for withdrawing money from ATMs. Remember that there is usually a charge (at least 2.5%) on ATM cash withdrawals abroad.

Changing Money

Exchange offices tend to offer better rates than banks. Reliable exchanges include **UAE Exchange** (☎04-229 7373; www.uaeexchange.com), which has multiple branches around town.

Credit Cards

Visa, MasterCard and American Express are widely accepted at shops, hotels and restaurants throughout Dubai. Debit cards are accepted at bigger retail outlets.

Tipping

By law, only food and beverage outlets in hotels are entitled to tack a service charge (usually 10%) onto bills. Independent restaurants are not officially permitted to do so, although many seem to thumb their nose at the regulation. If you are happy with the service, consider leaving an additional 5% to 10%.

Public Holidays

☑ **Top Tip** If you visit during Ramadan, don't forget there will be little drinking and dancing going on!

➡ Hejira is the Islamic New Year.

➡ Eid al-Fitr marks the end of Ramadan fasting and is a three-day celebration.

➡ Eid al-Adha is a four-day celebration following the main pilgrimage to Mecca, the hajj.

➡ Ramadan is the month during which Muslims fast during daylight hours.

➡ Prophet's Birthday varies annually according to the Islamic calendar; it's a one-day holiday for the public sector.

Safe Travel

We can't shout the following words loudly enough: do not attempt to carry illegal drugs into Dubai and/or use them while you are here. The drug laws are extremely strict and even a microscopic speck of a controlled substance could see you arrested. You must also ensure that medicines and drugs legal in your country are legal in Dubai before travelling with them. Having illegal substances in your bloodstream counts as possession too, and a urine test could see you found guilty.

Islamic Holidays

ISLAMIC YEAR	HEJIRA	PROPHET'S BIRTHDAY	RAMADAN	EID AL-FITR	EID AL-ADHA
1434 (2013)	4 Nov	24 Jan	9 Jul	8 Aug	15 Oct
1435 (2014)	4 Nov	13 Jan	28 Jun	28 Jul	4 Oct
1436 (2015)	25 Oct	24 Dec	18 Jun	17 Jul	23 Sep

Dos & Don'ts

➡ Don't swear, shout or make offensive hand gestures.

➡ Do always ask before taking a photo of locals.

➡ Don't get drunk in public places; it's unacceptable and severely punished.

➡ Don't point your finger or the soles of your feet towards locals.

➡ Do remove your shoes before entering the home of an Emirati.

➡ Do accept any hospitality offered; for example, coffee or dates.

➡ Don't bring up controversial topics, such as the Israeli-Palestinian conflict.

➡ Don't indulge in any public displays of affection (even holding hands).

➡ Do dress modestly outside the perimeters of your hotel or resort.

➡ Do wear swimwear at the beach, although nothing excessively skimpy.

In terms of safety for women, Dubai is one of the safest Middle Eastern destinations for female travellers. It is totally fine to take cabs and walk around on your own in most areas, although you might want to avoid the backstreets of Deira and Bur Dubai where you may attract unwanted male attention (although this would rarely be accompanied by any violence).

Telephone

☑ **Top Tip** Skype is blocked in the UAE, but many people get around this by downloading a proxy bypass or VPN.

➡ Local calls (within the same area code) are free.

➡ To phone another country from the UAE, dial ☎00 followed by the country code.

➡ To call the UAE, dial the country code ☎971.

Mobile Phones

The UAE's mobile-phone network uses the GSM 900 MHz and 1800 MHz standard. If you don't have a worldwide roaming service, consider buying a prepaid SIM card, available at the airport on arrival or at any number of city-wide stores.

Tourist Information

The **Department of Tourism & Commerce Marketing** (DTCM;

☎04-223 0000; www.dubai tourism.ae) operates 24-hour information kiosks in the Terminal 1 and 3 arrivals areas of Dubai International Airport, as well as booths at the following malls: Deira City Centre (Map p26), BurJuman (Map p42), Wafi Mall (Map p42) and Mercato Mall (Map p60).

Visas

At the time of writing, citizens of 34 countries get free on-the-spot visas on arrival in the UAE. Visas are valid for 30 days with an additional grace period of 10 days.

Check the www.dubai .ae website before you travel.

Language

MSA (Modern Standard Arabic) – the official lingua franca of the Arab world – and the everyday spoken version are quite different. The Arabic variety spoken in Dubai (and provided in this chapter) is known as Gulf Arabic.

Note that *gh* is a throaty sound (like the French 'r'), *r* is rolled, *dh* is pronounced as the 'th' in 'that', *th* as in 'thin', *ch* as in 'cheat' and *kh* as the 'ch' in the Scottish *loch*. The apostrophe (') indicates the glottal stop (like the pause in the middle of 'uh-oh'). Bearing these few points in mind and reading our pronunciation guides as if they were English, you'll be understood. The stressed syllables are indicated with italics. The markers (m) and (f) indicate masculine and feminine word forms respectively.

To enhance your trip with a phrasebook, visit **lonelyplanet.com**. Lonely Planet iPhone phrasebooks are available through the Apple App store.

Basics

Hello.
اهلا و سهلا. *ah*·lan was *ah*·lan

Goodbye.
مع السلامة. ma' sa·*laa*·ma

Yes./No.
نعم./لا. na·'am/la

Please.
من فضلك. min *fad*·lak (m)
من فضلك. min *fad*·lik (f)

Thank you.
شكراً. *shuk*·ran

Excuse me.
اسمح لي. is·*mah* lee (m)
اسمحي لي. is·mah·ee lee (f)

Sorry.
مع الاسف. ma' al·*as*·af

Do you speak English?
تتكلم/تتكلمي tit·*kal*·am/tit·*ka*·la·mee
انجليزية؟ in·glee·*zee*·ya (m/f)

I don't understand.
مو فاهم. moo *faa*·him

Eating & Drinking

I'd like (the) ..., please.
عطني/عطيني 'a·ti·nee/'a·*tee*·nee
الـ ... من فضلك. il ... min *fad*·lak (m/f)

bill	قائمة	*kaa*·'i·ma
drink list	قائمة	*kaa*·'i·mat
	المشروبات	il·mash·roo·*baat*
menu	الطعام	*kaa*·'i·mat
	قائمة	i·*ta*·'aam
that dish	الطبق	i·*tab*·ak
	هاذاك	*haa*·dhaa·ka

What would you recommend?
اش تنصح؟ aash *tan*·sah (m)
اش تنصحي؟ aash *tan*·sa·hee (f)

Do you have vegetarian food?
عندك طعم 'an·dak ta·'am
نباتي؟ na·*baa*·tee

Shopping

I'm looking for ...
مدور على ... moo·*daw*·ir 'a·la ... (m)
مدورة على ... moo·*daw*·i·ra 'a·la ... (f)

Can I look at it?
ممكن اشوف؟ *mum*·kin a·*shoof*

How much is it?
بكم؟ bi·*kam*

That's too expensive.
غالي جداً ghaa·lee jid·an

What's your lowest price?
اش السعر الاخر؟ aash i·si'r il·aa·khir

Do you have any others?
عندك اخرين؟ 'and·ak ukh·reen (m)
عندِك اخرين؟ 'and·ik ukh·reen (f)

Emergencies

Help!
مساعد! moo·saa·'id (m)
مساعدة! moo·saa·'id·a (f)

Call a doctor!
تصل/تِصلي ti·sil/ti·si·lee
على طبيب! 'a·la ta·beeb (m/f)

Call the police!
تصل/تِصلي ti·sil/ti·si·lee
على الشرطة! 'a·la i·shur·ta (m/f)

I'm lost.
انا ضعت a·na duht

I'm sick.
انا مريض. a·na ma·reed (m)
انا مريضة. a·na ma·ree·da (f)

Where are the toilets?
وين المرحاض؟ wayn il·mir·haad

Time & Numbers

What time is it?/At what time?
الساعة كم؟ i·saa·a' kam

It's/At (two) o'clock.
الساعة (ثنتين). i·saa·a' (thin·tayn)

yesterday ... البارح ... il·baa·rih ...
tomorrow ... باكر ... baa·chir ...
morning صباح sa·baah
afternoon بعد الظهر ba'd a·thuhr
evening مساء mi·saa

1	١	واحد	waa·hid
2	٢	اثنين	ith·nayn
3	٣	ثلاثة	tha·laa·tha
4	٤	اربع	ar·ba'
5	٥	خمسة	kham·sa
6	٦	ستة	si·ta
7	٧	سبعة	sa·ba'
8	٨	ثمانية	tha·maan·ya
9	٩	تسعة	tis·a'
10	١٠	عشرة	'ash·ar·a
100	١٠٠	مية	mee·ya
1000	١٠٠٠	الف	alf

Transport & Directions

Where's the ...?
من وين ...؟ min wayn ...

What's the address?
ما العنوان؟ ma il·'un·waan

Can you show me (on the map)?
لو سمحت law sa·maht
وريني wa·ree·nee
(علخريطة)؟ ('al·kha·ree·ta)

How far is it?
كم بعيد؟ kam ba·'eed

Please take me to (this address).
من فضلك خذني min fad·lak khudh·nee
(علعنوان هاذا). ('al·'un·waan haa·dha)

Please stop here.
لو سمحت law sa·maht
وقف هنا. wa·gif hi·na

What time's the bus?
الساعة كم a·saa·a' kam
الباص؟ il·baas

What station/stop is this?
ما هي maa hee·ya
المحطة هاذي؟ il·ma·ha·ta haa·dhee

Index

See also separate subindexes for:

⊗ **Eating p156**

◉ **Drinking p157**

★ **Entertainment p157**

🔒 **Shopping p157**

Behind the Scenes

Send Us Your Feedback

We love to hear from travellers – your comments help make our books better. We read every word, and we guarantee that your feedback goes straight to the authors. Visit **lonelyplanet.com/contact** to submit your updates and suggestions.

Note: We may edit, reproduce and incorporate your comments in Lonely Planet products such as guidebooks, websites and digital products, so let us know if you don't want your comments reproduced or your name acknowledged. For a copy of our privacy policy visit lonelyplanet.com/privacy.

Josephine's Thanks

Where to start? So many people provided me with invaluable help during my research trip. Top of the list has to be Richard and Angela Carey-Brown in Abu Dhabi, closely followed by Peter and Jan Casey who I shared many a meal and bottle of wine with in Dubai. I would also like to thank Brian Hollis, David Quinn, Farah Atoui from Art Dubai, Ilka Becker from Arabian Adventures, Sharmeen Sayed, Yasmine Behnam and Robin Chapman for his cat sitting and support. A mighty *shukran* to you all.

Acknowledgments

Cover photograph: Burj Khalifa, José Fuste Raga/Photolibrary.

Many of the images in this guide are available for licensing from Lonely Planet Images: www.lonelyplanetimages.com.

This Book

This 3rd edition of Lonely Planet's *Pocket Dubai* guidebook was researched and written by Josephine Quintero. The previous edition was written by Olivia Pozzan. Lara Dunston and Terry Carter wrote the 1st edition. This guidebook was commissioned in Lonely Planet's Melbourne office, and produced by the following:

Commissioning Editors Sam Trafford, William Gourlay **Coordinating Editors** Michelle Bennett, Kate James **Assisting Editor** Amy Karafin **Coordinating Cartographer** James Leversha **Coordinating Layout Designer** Adrian Blackburn **Managing Editors** Brigitte Ellemor, Annelies Mertens **Senior Editor** Susan Paterson

Managing Cartographers Shahara Ahmed, Adrian Persoglia **Managing Layout Designer & Internal Image Research** Jane Hart **Cover Research** Naomi Parker **Language Content** Branislava Vladisavljevic **Thanks to** Jessica Boland, Bruce Evans, Ryan Evans, Larissa Frost, Chris Girdler, Chris Love, Trent Paton, Kirsten Rawlings, Raphael Richards, Suzannah Shwer

Our Writer

Josephine Quintero

Josephine has enjoyed a long and varied career in journalism and travel writing, and has been a Lonely Planet author for several years. A UC Berkeley graduate, she worked on a wine magazine in the Napa Valley (California) before moving, ironically, to relatively 'dry' Kuwait. Josephine was editor of the *Kuwaiti Digest* (an oil-company magazine) there, during which time she travelled extensively throughout the Middle East and the Gulf, including the contrasting destinations of Yemen and Dubai. After being abruptly ousted from her home by Saddam Hussein's troops, she moved to Spain. She was delighted to have an opportunity to return to the Gulf and explore this extraordinary and tantalising destination in depth. Highlights on this trip included discovering the Deira souqs – along with avocado smoothies. Fabulous! Read more about Josephine at: lonelyplanet.com/members/ josephinequintero

Published by Lonely Planet Publications Pty Ltd
ABN 36 005 607 983
3rd edition – September 2012
ISBN 978 1 74179 822 7
© Lonely Planet 2012 Photographs © as indicated 2012
10 9 8 7 6 5 4 3
Printed in China

Although the authors and Lonely Planet have taken all reasonable care in preparing this book, we make no warranty about the accuracy or completeness of its content and, to the maximum extent permitted, disclaim all liability arising from its use.

All rights reserved. No part of this publication may be copied, stored in a retrieval system, or transmitted in any form by any means, electronic, mechanical, recording or otherwise, except brief extracts for the purpose of review, and no part of this publication may be sold or hired, without the written permission of the publisher. Lonely Planet and the Lonely Planet logo are trademarks of Lonely Planet and are registered in the US Patent and Trademark Office and in other countries. Lonely Planet does not allow its name or logo to be appropriated by commercial establishments, such as retailers, restaurants or hotels. Please let us know of any misuses: lonelyplanet.com/ip.